UN-DIETING™

Un-Doing the Diet Mentality…
And Staying Fit Forever!

UN-

DIETING™

A revolution begins..........

**by Jackie Jaye-Brandt, M.A., MFT
with Diana Lipson-Burge, R.D.**

ISBN: 1-4033-8441-X (ebook)
ISBN: 1-5872-1821-6 (Paperback)

This book is printed on acid free paper.

1stBooks – rev. 9/26/02

About the Book

The book *Un-Dieting* was born out a lifetime of failed diets, addiction to food and drugs, frustration over not having the body I always wanted to have, and ten years of experience working with eating disorders. After forty years of dieting, I finally learned that *diets* were the very thing *keeping* my weight on! Instinctively, I knew this must be true, not only from my own and my family's experience, but also, because I was finally beginning to see that all the weight I lost from diets was regained...sooner or later.

This book will teach you first, that there is only one way to gain weight...excess calories. Then you will learn that the main reason we eat excess calories is due to excess hunger, which is a direct result of *diets* and deprivation. Then I will show you why and how *we eat our emotions*, rather than expressing them. And most important, you will receive *tools*: tools for eliminating anger and resentment; tools for transforming fear and worry; and tools for communicating your wants and needs, so that you no longer have to eat your feelings. Lastly, you will notice that when you *have* self-esteem or confidence, you feel better, you perform better, you communicate better, your relationships are better, and your ability to lose excess weight is greatly enhanced. So, because self esteem goes hand in hand with success in every area of your life, you will receive 20 keys for raising your self-esteem on a daily basis.

Becoming liberated from diets is so empowering and so freeing that I truly believe you will find this to be the most exciting experience you've ever had...and one that will last a lifetime. I thank you for your courage in beginning this journey.

ACKNOWLEDGEMENTS

My wonderful parents, for your unrelenting faith in me, for your wisdom, your love, and for teaching and reminding me that anything is possible, I thank you and love you with all my heart.

My amazing husband, your love and respect for our relationship allows me to go out into the world and speak from my heart and from truth, and makes me credible. You are my constant sunshine and joy, and always the wind beneath my wings.

Diana, my deepest admiration, respect and gratitude for giving me the jigsaw-puzzle piece to enjoying food and trusting my body. What an incredible gift you've given me for life, and what a gift you are to the world.

Michael, my heartfelt thanks for getting inside my head and heart to put this all together for me. You are exactly what I asked the universe for, and I'm still astounded that I found you.

My best friends, Betsy and Annie. I thank you both for your total support of me, your willingness to do everything you could to make this possible, and your continuing love. I feel so incredibly lucky to have you both in my life.

Oprah, you have always been the inspiration for this book. I thank you for the daily reminder that I really can live the life I always dreamed.

Table of Contents

Part One

Facts you Must Know Before you can Understand the Psychology of Weight Loss

Chapter One -- Welcome to Un-Dieting!

When I was filling out my application to become a psychotherapist and came to the question "Have you ever been arrested for a crime?", I remember picking up the phone without thinking, calling my best friend, and saying "Do you, by any chance, remember how many times I got arrested?...was it three or four?"! There was a moment of silence, and then a belly laugh that to this day only *she* can evoke in me, and then I said "Good Lord, will I ever escape my pathetic past?!" Among other things my friend told me that day, she said to stop *suffering* with my past, and to instead *use* it to help others. I didn't really understand what she was saying until many years later.

My problems began when I was 12 years old and started stealing diet pills from a huge bottle of Dexedrine in my mother's closet (eating disorders are quite often passed down). I remember she called them her *happy pills,* and I'm sure that *label* had an impact on me too. I always felt fatter than the *popular* girls (which was a conclusion drawn from an incident that happened to me at age 4), and the bottom line was that I thought that if I could just get skinny, I could be popular too. I never did get to that feeling of popular, and no matter how thin I got, I never *felt* skinny. But those pills....I really liked those pills. Not surprisingly, what followed was a twenty-year battle with anorexia, disordered eating, and a major addiction to drugs.

The drugs were a *loud* and distracting cover-up for my addiction to food. There were huge food addiction and obesity issues in my family, and I was going to make sure that I didn't become *one of them*. I clearly chose drugs and several near-death experiences over the possibility of being what-I-considered-to-be *fat*. There have numerous times in my life that I should have been killed and wasn't, and I am now clear that I am *supposed* to be here to help others. This book is my opportunity to do that.

I am pleased to tell you that I pulled myself out of a life that felt like it was spinning out of control, went back to school at age 39 and became an *Organizational Psychotherapist*. I teach company owners and executives how to create a *team* with their employees, and how to create a place where everyone wants to work and contribute toward goals. I am also a *Lecturer,* specializing in teaching the skills for powerful communication, self-esteem, and skills for tapping into the power of the mind (all the things I needed to learn for myself). I also teach people how to master fear, anger and stress, so that they no longer have to *eat* their feelings. I noticed that the biggest problem in people's relationships is their *need to be right*, so I teach people how to break free from the constraints of that need. Lastly, I discovered the psychology of why people eat and gain weight. And then, with the help of my colleague, whom I'm about to introduce, I learned how to eat in a way that totally satisfies me, keeps me lean, and eliminates dieting. Most important to me, it makes perfect sense.

Here's my colleague, Diana, summing up her story:

I can still remember the sight and smell of the green oxygen tanks that were hooked up to my mother's bed as she and I shared ice cream while she was dying of breast cancer. In the last few weeks of her life she could no longer talk, and sharing ice cream was our unspoken way of bonding during our remaining time together, as well as our daily ritual. After she died I never stopped eating ice cream. For most of my life I never saw the connection between my love for ice cream and the loss of my mother. I thought ice cream was simply my secret addiction. It was here, at age four, that I first learned to handle my emotions through food."

Diana became bulimic and anorexic for the next twelve years. To educate me on how pervasive the conditions of anorexia and bulimia had become around the country, she told me that when she attended a college in Nebraska, school officials in the female dormitories had to lock the bathrooms after meals, because the sewer system couldn't handle the back-up of vomit!

Diana began studying nutrition. Her main motivation, she says, was that here was another way to get *more* information on how to get *thin*, which basically was *another diet*. But over the last fourteen years of treating and specializing in eating disorders, the outcome is that she has developed powerful, yet

4

amazingly-simple notions that will absolutely change your relationship to food and eating. While we wrote this book together, Diana delivered her first child, Jennifer; and amongst the myriad of miracles she experienced came the realization that she *knows* she has *beaten* her disordered eating! This is something we both believe to be a miracle, especially given the sad, low percentage of people who recover, and for those who do, the long, intensive journey it takes.

With the help of Diana, I have personally recovered from a lifetime of failed diets, food addiction, drug addiction and deprivation mentality. I've learned how to get to my natural body weight and stay there. I've learned how to *view* myself differently... and to stop *comparing* myself to other people. By doing this, I was able to get a *realistic* idea of what is possible for *my* particular body. I learned that food should not be an *enemy* or something to be feared. It should be enjoyed and savored, like all great moments in our lives. I learned that the body does *not want* to be overweight and uncomfortable. The *body* wants to be lean and efficient, in its own particular way. And I learned how to develop a relationship with food that is so amazingly-different from the way it used to be, and so freeing and liberating, that I feel passionate about sharing it with others.

The reason we *came together* with this effort was simple. Diana realized that no matter *what* tools she gave people, if they didn't love themselves, they would sabotage their own efforts.... every time! We must understand that *self-esteem* is at the core of *everything* we do. You will notice that **there is a direct and proportionate relationship between your self-esteem and your results**. This means that if you look at your life, you will notice that in any area where you are really *great* at something, you will also see that you have high self-esteem (or self-confidence) in that area. In areas where your self-esteem is low, you can usually count on your results being low (at least to yourself). What this means is that **if you have *no self-esteem* in regard to your weight and your body--- meaning you don't believe you will ever look the way you want to--- you will end up with *no results.***

To explain it fully takes some time, but is well worth it. The first four chapters have to be the *facts* about real weight gain, because most people have years and years of misguided notions to *dump* before they can take in the factual dynamics between food, eating, satiation (satisfaction, or fullness) and weight gain. After that, I will teach you how to uncover *beliefs* about yourself, food, and weight that can actually *keep* weight on. I will show you the connection between *fear, worry* and weight gain. I will show you how the way you *talk to yourself* can produce the results you want with your weight. I will show you how to *forgive* yourself and other people in your life. (Whether or not you choose to *use* the tools I give you will be a huge factor in your outcome!) I will also teach you how to get *complete* with people and situations in your life, so that you no longer have to *carry* those situations along with you (in your mind). I will then teach you how to *release anger appropriately*, so that you no longer have to *eat* your anger. I will show you how you can give up *needing to be right*, which is very, very freeing. And lastly, I will give you the 20 Keys to *Self-Esteem*, so that you can *keep* your body at its lean and comfortable self for the rest of your life.

If you're ready, I'm ready to take you take you through a journey of understanding the psychology and the facts surrounding body weight and body image, and all I need from you is the willingness to take an exploration into your own mind, so that you can work *with* it instead of *against* it. I applaud you for your courage in taking this journey.

Understanding the Dynamics

The first thing we want to understand is that Americans are getting heavier and heavier, and we're trying diet after diet, without any lasting success. There are some very clear reasons for this, and they aren't really about *food*. Most of the reasons are psychological in nature, such as *inability to express anger, crippling fear, incompletions from the past, lack of communication skills,* and *faulty belief systems;* but these feelings *manifest* themselves through physical eating. If and when we can get to these underlying psychological issues, explore them, and then transform them by using practical tools, our eating will then shift naturally.

To understand how we learned to *stuff* our feelings, you might want to first ask yourself some simple questions:

When was the last time you looked in your mirror and said *something* like this to yourself: "I'm beautiful and wonderful, and my body just seems to get better every day!"?!

When was the last time any one of your friends or loved ones told you that *they* said something like that to themselves in the mirror?

And when was the last time you noticed little groups of people at work all talking about how wonderful *they* are?!

If you answered "never" or are still laughing at these questions, think about this next one: When was the last time you looked in your mirror and said, "I hate my body, I hate my face, I hate my fat?"!

If you answered this last question much more easily than the first two, you are like most people. Most of us criticize ourselves unmercifully, while we rarely acknowledge or accentuate our positives or our achievements.

But let's think about this logically for a minute. Why is it so easy for us to hate ourselves and our bodies...and so difficult to love ourselves? And does this make any sense?!

If you are a mom or dad, I know you don't want to teach this to your children, but this is *exactly* what children are learning. America's largest majority of anorexics and bulimics are adolescents. We have a country filled with girls and boys, women and men, who hate themselves and their bodies, who are consistently dissatisfied with what they have and the way things are, and who feel compelled to compare themselves constantly with people who have thinner bodies and more material things than they have! Children are not happy with the image they see in the mirror. One of the reasons for this is that mom and dad have probably never been happy with their image, and probably none of their peers are happy either. There is a lot of *agreement* for this faulty behavior.

7

It is not your fault. Nobody has ever taught us the basics of loving ourselves. When was the last time you saw a class offered, "Loving Yourself 101"?! We place very small value on a concept that really needs to be a number one priority. I have found that it is virtually impossible to truly love another human being until we have learned to truly love ourselves. *Until we learn to love ourselves, we seek people who will give us love; Until we learn to understand ourselves, we seek people with whom we can feel understood; Until we learn to just be ourself, we will seek people around whom we can most be ourself.* In other words, it is essential for us as human beings to find a way to get our self-worth from inside ourself so that we don't have to keep *needing* validation from others. Besides, how long after someone acknowledges us do we stay satisfied before we need another charge from another person? If we don't get this worth from inside, then it is easy to become an empty vessel that can never be filled up for very long.

Another reason we need to get esteem from inside ourselves is so that we can ward off all the negativity, pessimism, and competitiveness that comes our way. When other people try to bring us down, or suck us into their negative world, it is with self-induced self-esteem that we can gather the strength to say, "No, I won't let you do that to me".

Now let's add another piece to this puzzle of our persistent weight problem: It is important to understand that throughout the decades, until the 1960's, *thinness* in women has historically made *brief* appearances. In the late 1880's women began looking for more definition to their bodies. In the 1890's there was new interest being paid to the female derriere. 1904 was the year of the corset, where focus was shifted to the waistline and breasts. In 1908 Paul Poiret, a clothing designer, shifted people's visual attention to long legs and a flat chest. The 1920's saw another brief appearance of thinness for the *flapper* era, which was followed by three decades of the voluptuous woman.

In the 1950's women were more interested in comparing their breasts to those of other women, rather than being concerned about their weight. The average woman was a size 14, and the average movie star wasn't far from this. Marilyn

Monroe, the sex goddess of the 50's was a size 12. There was an episode of *I Love Lucy* where Ricky promised Lucy a spot in his nightclub show only if she could get herself into a size 12 costume after delivering their baby. At least during this time, the average woman was comparing her body to something that was fairly attainable! Women have always seeked models with whom they could compare themselves --- not a good thing to do ever, but we do it --- And at least here women felt like they *had a chance* in the competition for men, marriage and sex.

But it was the 1960's that brought the beginning of America's preoccupation with slimness as a *persistent* condition, rather than *episodic*! It would be the beginning of *four decades* of dieting, women comparing themselves to what is genetically unattainable for the *average* female, and consistent dissatisfaction with the human body, the way it was originally packaged.

A 1995 psychological study found that spending just three minutes thumbing through a fashion magazine caused seventy percent of women to feel *depressed, guilty and shameful.* The fact is that only a tiny percentage of the population is born with genetics that make it possible to wear a size three, but media bombardment of images of thin women are forcing an entire country to aim for a size that isn't humanly possible for most females! And because starving ourselves isn't working -- we're still not getting into that size three --- it makes us feel depressed, worthless, isolated...a sure signal for a food binge!

And since this condition has been going on for so long, it is getting worse. You can see it in subtle and overt ways. For example, size three, the smallest size carried in clothing stores for thirty years, is no longer small enough for upcoming anorexics. We now have a size zero!

Deciding to be rail-slim is somewhat like deciding to become shorter! It's trying to change something that nature simply won't permit to be changed. Let's examine how this sets us up to feel consistently dissatisfied with ourselves. The media is run by the advertisers...and the advertisers are mainly the multi-billion dollar beauty and weight industry. This massive industry encompasses diet centers, diet food, diet pills, jewelry, hair, make-up, plastic surgery, vitamins, and various related goods and services. Every time you look at a magazine filled with models who are rail-thin (usually with surprisingly large breasts), the media makes you hate your body just a little bit more.

It's what you see all day long. It's on TV. It's on advertisements, on billboards, and on the sides of buses. It hits you when you walk into a shopping mall, look through a newspaper, or watch a movie. First, they make us dissatisfied with what we are. Then, they cash in on that dissatisfaction.

It's not their fault. They're simply a reflection of *us*. If we didn't buy the whole package, they wouldn't be selling it. The fashion industry has the task of convincing you to throw out perfectly good clothes each year because they're "out of style." The hair and make-up industries must make us believe that if we're better looking, we'll have a happier life. And the diet industry makes billions each year with their meal plans and special foods that keep people chasing the impossible dream. The dream is that some diet can make people and keep people incredibly thin--and thus appealing.

I'm not writing solely as a therapist and expert in the psychology of food addiction. As I explained before, I was completely hooked into this syndrome myself. I always believed that the right pill, the right diet, and some willpower would work. It never did. I was always battling a distorted body image. When I say *distorted body image*, I mean that whenever I looked in the mirror, all I ever saw was fat. The fat was so magnified in my mind that I had a constant visual image of a giant balloon that kept getting bigger and bigger. And if, on rare occasions, I were to shift from hating my fat thighs, I would simply move to hating my fat butt, or my fat stomach, or some other part of my anatomy that wasn't okay with me.

I lived with a nonstop preoccupation with being attractive and wanting to fit in. I had this fantasy image that I kept wanting to slide into; and as the years passed and the image got further and further from my reach, I would discover something new that would give me hope... plastic surgery. "Now", I thought, "if I can just have enough fat removed, I can *finally*

10

become my fantasy image." Unfortunately, there's a huge problem with fantasies...they're fantasies! They never come true. But even worse, they *set us up* for disappointment. We need to get rid of our fantasy images, and instead get real about our individual bodies and souls.

I'm going to confirm for you what you've heard from many people and always suspected...diets never work! They might work for a while--a few weeks, months, even a year. But everyone knows what happens. The weight comes back, slowly at first, and then with blinding speed. So what do most people do? First they hate themselves, and then they...GO ON ANOTHER DIET! People often tell Diana and me, "I'm going back to my Diet Center," or "back to my grapefruit diet," or "back to my 'protein-only' diet." When we ask why, they answer, "because it worked!" Well, if it worked, why do they have to go back and do it again?! But they do, and each time, they think, "*This* time it will work!" In fact, most people feel that it's "right" to be on a diet and "wrong" not to.

So they lose some weight; and gain back more.

And they hate themselves all over again.

The problem isn't that people are picking the wrong diet. All diets are just recycled and repackaged versions of earlier diets. And it's not your so-called lack of willpower. The problem is that diets are *doomed* to fail. It has never been your fault that diets haven't worked for you. You are simply being sold a bill of goods by a *multi-billion-dollar diet industry* that depends on people not feeling okay the way they are, and depends on our continuing belief that we "just haven't found the right diet."

I struggled with the idea of writing this book and turning it over to a publishing industry that would place it in the "diet" section of bookstores--because this is not a diet book. It's the Un-Diet book! It's the antithesis of a diet book because it will show you how dieting is the very thing that keeps us gaining weight. Nevertheless, I'm comforted by the fact that even though you may find it in the "diet" section, I know that after reading it, you will never want or need to diet again!

I will show you how to eat in a way that honors your body and fills you up physically, not emotionally. I will show you how to get your emotional needs met through something other than food. I will also show you how to avoid the "Quiet Diet Riot"--the terrible backlash of weight gain that comes from dieting and depriving oneself of certain foods and then overeating because of that deprivation. I'll show you *why* you've been overeating and untrustworthy around food, and I'll show you why it's not your fault.

This book is not just about food and diet. It is, above all else, about *self-love*. You will receive practical tools for raising your self-esteem on a daily basis, and you will fall in love with yourself, maybe for the first time. You will see that loving yourself is not only selfless, but is *essential* before you can truly give love to others, because you can't give away what you don't have yourself. You'll see that you've learned to *minimize* yourself, point out your weaknesses, be a good mother and a "nice" person...but you have never learned how to create self-love on a daily basis.

You'll learn that there is a way to maneuver through life and *handle* all that is thrown at you in a functional and productive way, without having so much *drama* around everything. You'll finally be able to feel your feelings...without needing to stuff them. Clients often tell me how scary it is to think about feeling those feelings they've never wanted to feel before. I say it's scarier to keep trying to stuff them with food. They learn-- as will you--that those feelings are not powerful enough to kill us, or even do harm. In fact, right after we feel them fully, we start to feel liberated!

Since fear and anger are such giant emotions, they gobble up feelings of happiness, sexuality, and exuberance. I will teach you how to express anger appropriately, how to transform fear, and how to change your belief systems so that your mind *works* for you, rather than *running* you.

My painful history of extremely low self-esteem propelled me to learn about and teach others how to build and maintain their self-esteem. I have learned that with self-esteem we can do *anything* we want in life. It enhances our communication, our relationships, how we *take in* information, everything. When you learn how to build it yourself, you will be amazed at the difference it makes in every day of your life.

Today, at age fifty, I weigh pretty much within a few pounds of what I weighed when I was in my twenties. I say "pretty much" because I no longer weigh myself. (And soon, I hope, neither will you!) I am no longer at the mercy of a bathroom scale--a mindless metal object that people use in order to determine how they feel! Today I look in the mirror and see a beautiful woman who is really okay in every way. My weight is no longer a concern to me, and food is a joy, rather than something to be feared. Can you imagine how much fun it is to feel this way?! And can you imagine what great things follow when you feel this good about yourself?!

I know you've heard this before, but it's an amazing irony that's very hard to believe: as soon as we can allow ourselves to be esteemed, admirable, and okay, just the way we are now, the weight seems to fall away. This, however, is an extremely difficult thing for people to grasp when they've spent a lifetime believing that they are not okay..."until I lose this weight," "until I'm successful," "until I can stop failing at everything I do," and on and on and on.

Could you entertain the possibility that "Un-Dieting" could be the solution to your eating problems? Can you see that this "dieting--then binge--then dieting" mentality isn't working and doesn't make sense? Can you see that food shouldn't have to be an obsession?

For the next two months, would you be willing to give your trust to this program, and suspend your beliefs about what works, no matter how much you think you need the rigidity of the "right" diet? If so, read on, because I'm certain that you will find this to be the most exciting, enlightening and freeing experience you've ever had, and one that you will surely want for the rest of your life!

Chapter Two
The Birth of an Eating Disorder

Infants aren't shy about being hungry. Why are we? Infants do not have eating disorders. All infants cry when they are hungry, approximately every three to four hours. In most homes, they are quickly offered food. They then eat until satisfied, no more, no less. And they usually make it really clear that they have finished--by turning their head away from the food, handing the spoon back to mom, or, in some instances, clearing the whole tray onto the floor!

As infants, we were clearly in touch with our hunger and clearly in touch with being satisfied. We repeated this process each day, every three to four hours, crying for food, without concern from mom that perhaps this was too many times a day to be fed. This happened for several years until someone decided to override our innate instincts by saying something like, "No, you're not hungry yet...you'll spoil your appetite for dinner."

What happens when our parents and authority figures override our innate ability to eat when we're hungry and stop when we're full? We become programmed to believe that we don't really know what we want...that our natural instincts are incorrect. In this process we are reprogrammed to rely on someone other than ourselves to determine how much we should eat and when we should eat.

....

Truth Number One: **infants (and all other human beings) naturally get hungry every three to four hours.**
Truth Number Two: **when infants feel satiated, they stop eating.**

....

We get further separated from our natural instincts with phrases like "Wait 'til your father gets home" or "Why can't you get on *our* schedule?" We stop believing that we know best about when it's time to eat and we learn to trust only external cues about hunger. Yet when we examine these external cues, we find that they are *ludicrous and make no sense*. Each time we pay attention to those external cues, we become further and further divorced from natural instincts about eating...until all those instincts are extinct!

Fortunately, infants (unlike their older but less wise counterparts) tend to be very resistant to this process. After crying, being fed, and then determining that they are full, it is extremely difficult to get them to eat more. Coaxing and prodding usually gets ignored or resisted, and most infants are simply done eating, ready to move onto the next item of business. The infant does not care if there are three bites left in the jar. The infant does not care about whether or not that is wasteful. The infant does not care about whether other infants are starving in other parts of the world. The infant...is full.

In some families, the infant's cries indicating hunger pangs are totally disregarded, sometimes in favor of a schedule more convenient to the parent, and sometimes because of scarcity of food and financial straits. In these instances the child may grow up feeling trepidation that there won't be enough. This can, of course, lead to overeating and overcompensating for the possibility of scarcity.

As a brand-new mom, my "Un-Dieting" colleague, Diana, is just beginning to realize the awesome responsibility parents take on, and we both certainly understand why well-meaning parents may want to coax infants into eating a few more bites, perhaps to "finish the jar" so they'll grow "big and strong." From the standpoint of any parent, this seems logical. We probably learned this from our own well-meaning parents. From the standpoint of the dietitian specializing in eating disorders, however, this is number one on the list of what NOT to do and is one of the primary reasons underlying eating disorders in people of all ages. If you have done this with your children, don't beat yourself up over it. I think everybody does it...*just don't ever do it again!*

Let's return to that poor, confused kid we were discussing a moment ago. That child now faces our society-wide tradition of "three square meals at fixed mealtimes every single day." (Where'd <u>that</u> come from, by the way?) Fixed mealtimes of breakfast, lunch and dinner occur at intervals dictated by forces other than our innate feelings of hunger. Eventually, our inborn ability to know when we are hungry and to stop when we are full is lost. As infants and children, we get admonished for not eating breakfast at seven thirty a.m., lunch at noon and dinner at six p.m. We get admonished for snacking in between. We get admonished for not finishing everything on our plate. And the instinct that once told us when to eat and when to stop is destroyed.

Listen to the story of my client Jennifer, a thirty-two year old financial services professional in Los Angeles:

"For me, somewhere around age six, things changed in my house. My stepmother was busy attending to other things, and apparently I wasn't her only priority. I would tell her that I was hungry, and remember hearing her respond, 'No, you're not...you'll spoil your appetite,' or 'Your father will be home at six, and then we'll eat.' For most children that age, mom and dad are gods. Though I was dumbfounded initially by her response, I thought mom and dad knew better than me. I made a seemingly small, subconscious decision at age six that I couldn't trust myself to know when I was really hungry.

"Even though I kept trying to get food, and told her on many other occasions that I was hungry, I received similar responses, affirming again that I didn't really know when I was hungry. Never did I hear my step-mom ask me to 'check in' with my hunger scale, the same hunger scale that caused me to cry, and subsequently get fed every three to four hours, a few years earlier. So, age six was when I began to conclude that I was untrustworthy in regard to my hunger. In addition, I began to live in a private world of secretly eating when no one was around."

You can see that at a very young age we are stripped of our intuitive power to discern our hunger, and instead we learn to eat by time on a clock. This is critical to understand, because it explains not only how we came to be out of touch with true hunger, but also demystifies our propensity to turn to food for things other than hunger. We may turn anger into a desire to eat. We may do the same thing when we feel loneliness, boredom, disappointment or exhaustion.

Let me explain. If we have grown up using food and hunger to <u>avoid</u> the bigger and scarier emotions of fear and anger, then we will actually create a strong connection in the brain between fear, anger, and eating to avoid or deny that uncomfortableness, and that then becomes a well-travelled pathway in our brain. Subsequently, every time we're faced with these uncomfortable emotions, we will eat simply because this is our well-travelled pathway, not because we're hungry.

When we keep doing this over and over through life, much like a well-travelled road that we become accustomed to taking...it becomes where our brain goes to naturally. We literally carve neurological pathways in the brain. Then we eat instead of facing our fears and we eat instead of confronting our anger. Eating becomes the more easily accessible response through force of habit. In short, eating becomes the standard way of dealing with life, rather than handling the feelings that the eating is covering.

....

Eating becomes the standard way of dealing with life, rather than handling the feelings that the eating is covering

....

In addition, that intriguing combination of breakfast, lunch, and dinner means we're supposed to be hungry only three times a day. But are we? No! Most workers are expected to eat between noon and two p.m. every day, whether they're hungry or not. Add to this a disturbing fact that most people work until at least five or six p.m., and many work until much later, which means they probably don't eat dinner until approximately seven hours after their lunch!   People will break down in my office and confide their embarrassment at being so hungry that they devour their food. Of course they devour... they're starving!

I tell my clients that discovering--relearning, actually--the innate ability of a child to discern his or her own hunger will help them understand that they were born with this ability to be intuitive about food. (Intuitive about *everything*, really, but in this book we're talking about eating.)   When did *you* lose *your* innate ability to choose food for sustenance?

18

Can you remember when you started to eat for other reasons? Was there a painful incident or a series of events?

Almost sixty percent of our overeating clients were molested as children. If you have molestation in your background and have not dealt with that molestation, you will probably need more than this book. I would suggest a trained professional. But even if you've had the courage to find a therapist or caring professional with whom to discuss those events, you may not have recognized the connection between the molestation and the loss of your ability to gauge your own true hunger for food.

Or perhaps there is nothing specific and traumatic to point to--nothing as dramatic and horrible as molestation. Perhaps you have a childhood memory of always being hungry for...something.

Please take a few minutes and think back to the earliest time when you weren't permitted to be intuitive about your hunger? Don't be afraid of this, or put it off until later. The feelings won't hurt you. In fact, they will start to heal you. Do you remember when you first lost that special power? Let's get to the essence of why you may be out of touch with your gift for "intuitive eating."

Exercise:

Write down your earliest memory of using food to handle other emotions, or the first time you remember eating because of something other than hunger.

_____

_____

_____

_____

_____

_____

_____

_____

_____

_____

_____

_____

_____

_____

_____

_____

_____

Finding the Key

As an adult who lost track years ago of my own gift for intuitive eating, I had become a professional dieter. I was always restricting food and was so nervous about gaining weight that I put all my energy into smoking cigarettes. Whenever I started thinking about food, I simply planned and plotted how I would sneak away to have a cigarette somewhere, without anyone knowing. I couldn't quit smoking, though I tried hundreds of times....but I was a controlled eater.

In addition to buying every new and improved diet and doing them religiously, I learned how to restrict myself from eating egg yokes, butter, cheese and desserts. I was always so proud when I ordered food, because I sounded so virtuous ... egg-white omelets, pizzas without cheese, diet coke. Everyone told me how good I was. I liked that. The only problem was that my diet was *boring!* So incredibly *boring* that eventually, when no one was around I would binge, and then I'd eat all the things I had been deprived of...cookies, chocolate, and ice cream.

I was always alone, and I always ate fast...needing to stuff it in quickly before anyone could see. I would then feel fat, alone, and guilty. I vowed I would get back to controlling myself again tomorrow.

After all these failed efforts to control my eating, I had a massive breakthrough. I came to understand that if I'm *really* going to keep weight off, *there can't be any forbidden foods*! I didn't realize that avoiding foods causes us to overeat them when we finally get near them! I always believed that if I were allowed to eat chocolate chip cookies, my favorite food, I would never be able to stop. Clearly, I might just as well set up camp at Mrs. Fields! I had to learn that it was *okay to eat what I wanted,* as long as I followed some basic guidelines about satisfying my hunger, and as long as I learned to trust myself that when I'd had enough I'd stop.

Just as infants know when they are full, so do we adults. It's about learning to trust that our inner voice will say, "Okay, that's all the cookies I need for right now. I don't really have to finish the whole bag."

The reason we've been untrustworthy around our favorite food is that when we get around it we're usually *way too hungry*. Add to that the fact that we haven't had it in so long, we end up devouring it... and feeling bad. That self-starvation isn't our own inner wisdom. It's not even the voice in our head telling us to go hungry. It's the voice of the dietocracy, the voice of a well-meaning parent telling us not to eat when we're hungry *now* or to "clean our plate" when we're already full. It's even the voice of the nineteenth century factory boss who has to keep the production line moving...and therefore can't let his workers eat anytime but when the noon lunch whistle blows. The Un-Diet is about learning to recognize that these voices *aren't* our inner wisdom about our own needs for eating. It's about recognizing that it's okay to eat when we're hungry...and to eat what our body requests.

So when clients tell me that they can't trust themselves around food, I remind them that their way--dieting--isn't working. And they all know that thin people eat until they feel like stopping. They do not deprive themselves of foods they like.

And doesn't it feel logical that your own body can signal you when to stop eating? It's just a question of *learning to listen for, and to, those Stop signals.*

Here's how it worked for me. First, Diana explained that I must no longer declare any foods as "forbidden." I could eat those chocolate chip cookies every day--but with these two critically important points in mind. First, I always had to make sure I wasn't too hungry when it was "cookie time." Also, I had to make sure I was balancing those cookies with some protein at that feeding (a new word we will to replace *meals*). I didn't feel convinced...but I gave it a try.

The first week, I stopped at Mrs. Fields for chocolate chip cookies every day. I ate one or two cookies each time, and remember feeling scared that I would definitely do this every day--and balloon up to three hundred pounds. Though I wasn't supposed to weigh myself, I did, and was shocked that I didn't gain any weight. The cookie binge lasted for about two weeks, whereupon, believe it or not, I actually became slightly bored with cookies. I noticed that when I allowed myself to have cookies every day, that I *approached the cookies differently.* To put it simply, the cookies lost their power over me once they stopped being "forbidden foods."

On the "Un-Diet," when you allow yourself to eat the forbidden food, the food transforms into something else (it is no longer a demon in your mind), and you move on from it. It's brilliantly simple. Face the food head on and allow it to be like any other food (with one exception: don't face it when you're too hungry!) This concept probably goes against every rule of dieting you've ever heard. I was much more comfortable when someone or some diet told me exactly what I could and couldn't eat, and you probably feel the same way.

On the "Un-Diet," we're advocating that nothing is forbidden!

Now it's time for the next big step on the Un-Diet--*it's time to get rid of your bathroom scale.* Let's talk about why you don't need it anymore--and why you *never needed it in the first place.*

First of all, bathroom scales are notoriously inaccurate as measurers of the human body. The body weight of all men and women fluctuates anywhere between one and seven pounds over the course of the average month! This fluctuation has *nothing to do* with whether you're sticking to some diet. It's a function of many things--including fluid intake; salt intake; if you're female, where you are in your monthly cycle; barometric pressure, dehydration, and many other things. So "weighing in" on any given morning never gives an accurate snapshot of what we *really* weigh. Your scale does not and cannot provide an accurate reflection of what's really going on with your body or your eating!

....

Your scale does not and cannot provide an accurate reflection of what's really going on with your body or your eating!

....

You will learn in Chapter Four exactly how one pound of fat is formed on the body. What is important to know right now is that a scale is not an accurate measure of one's true weight. In addition, no two people are the same. Every body frame is different. No two people can ever or should ever be compared, since we are all inherently different.

Next, let me ask you this: who really cares what you weigh? Think about it: When was the last time someone asked you how much you weigh? Do you know the exact weight of any of your friends? Your loved ones? Why do we obsess about a number that no one else cares about?

When I was in my twenties, for some mysterious reason, the idea of weighing 117 pounds sounded perfect to me. To this day, my driver's license reflects this number. Why 117? Why not 118 or 111? I have no idea. But 117 was my magic number, and if I tipped the scales over that number, I was in misery until I could starve myself back below it. Does that make any sense to you? The fact is that your body has a natural *range* of weight that's healthy and ideal...just for you. Everybody...every *body*...is different. It doesn't make sense to be at the tyranny of bathroom scales, or insurance company average weight charts, or anything else.

··

**By practicing Un-Dieting, you'll weigh *what your body wants
to weigh,* not some random number that someone else put on
a chart to suit you and everyone else in the world with your
height.**

··

By the way, all those insurance company weight charts
reflect an evolution toward thinner and thinner, just like the
models we see in ads. The 1950's charts actually reflected
women being weighed in high heels! Those silly weight charts,
along with bathroom scales and our advertising culture, all
promote the idea that we aren't healthy unless we're super-thin
and weighing what a chart says we should weigh. And that's
just not true. The proof is that so many women (and men) are
dying of anorexia because they've bought this nonsense that thin
equals beautiful. Super-thin really just means one
bulemic/anorexic/unhappy person trying to fit into what most
people aren't meant to be.

Another reason for getting rid of our bathroom scales is the
insidious thought process that scales provoke. It works this way:
we eat something we label as "bad." We're convinced that we'll
see the result in the form of increased weight...the very next
morning. Even if you were *trying*, it would be extremely
difficult to gain a pound of fat...or a pound of *anything*... in a
day. During the years that the Raiders played football in Los
Angeles, my colleague Diana worked with the team as a diet
consultant. She learned from working with football players that
*not even three hundred pound linemen can put on a pound of fat
in a day!* If the Raiders can't do that, surely you can't.

Ah, but you may be saying, what about the time I gained
three pounds after I went to that big Thanksgiving dinner? The
answer is surprising: just because your scale recorded more
weight *doesn't mean you got heavier.* As I mentioned earlier,
the human body fluctuates one to seven pounds every month,
depending on a series of factors known and unknown. Just
because the scale gives you a higher number doesn't mean you
gained weight. The scale isn't smart enough to measure changes

in your fluid intake, salt intake, barometric pressure, your menstrual cycle, let alone the factors researchers haven't yet identified. We're trained to believe that scales know our bodies better than we do. It's time to dismiss that inaccurate notion and trust ourselves again.

....

We're trained to believe that scales know our bodies better than we do. It's time to dismiss that inaccurate notion and trust ourselves again.

....

Some of my clients have an opposite situation with their bathroom scale. They go to a party, eat a lot, and drink a lot of alcohol. The next morning comes...the reckoning. They gingerly step on the scale...they just *know* they're fatter than ever...they scrunch their eyes shut...they work up their courage...and they look down at the magic number. And by God, it's lower! What do they tell themselves? They ate, they drank...and they *GOT AWAY WITH IT!*

No, maybe not. Alcohol dehydrates the body. If you drink booze and step on the scale the next day, you're likely to see the results of your dehydration, not the results of your diet. But wait a few days. Eventually, the scale will register a weight gain, whether real or connected to that monthly weight cycle I just described. What happens then? We get frustrated and say, "See? This diet isn't working." That's when we throw in the towel...and eat everything in sight, out of frustration, out of disappointment, out of rage that we blew yet another diet.

Since we *believe* we've gained weight, we're likely to *feel* bloated. Our subconscious mind then has to make us right. If we believe we're heavier, our mind will see to it that we *get* heavier. If we believe we've blown a diet "one more time," will we feel motivated to eat well today, to exercise, to feel good about ourselves, to trust that our body is doing the right thing at all times? Of course not. And that's when we *really* gain weight--by overeating--after we convince ourselves that nothing we're doing is working. And we have evidence in the form of

25

that metallic object in the bathroom taunting us every single morning.

Bodybuilders and athletes tell themselves "No pain, no gain." I've got one for you: "No scale, no fail."

....

Bodybuilders and athletes tell themselves "No pain, no gain."
I've got another one:
No scale, no fail.

....

So throw away your bathroom scale. It's not telling you anything accurate or useful about yourself. It makes you feel bad about yourself, and obsessed with food, dieting, and weight, every time you even notice it, let alone the times you actually step onto it.

Obsessing about food and weight actually diverts us from the real problems in our lives that need addressing, like the wrong job or career; untreated alcoholism; a dead-end marriage. By giving up the scale, we surrender one of the central props in the ongoing *drama* of our weight. Get rid of the scale...and *live.* I will also teach you how to think trim and healthy, so that your body can follow your mind.

When you step out and **dare** to try the "Un-Diet", just remember that the rest of the nation is still trying diet after diet...and gaining more and more weight. Before I can explain to you why the "Un-Diet" really works, we need to understand why all the regular diets fail so consistently. That's the subject of the next chapter.

Chapter Three -- Why We're Gaining Weight

There are four basic reasons why we are dieting more...and gaining weight anyway. In this chapter we'll look at each of the four reasons in turn.

REASON #1: THE QUIET DIET RIOT

When you deprive yourself of a certain "forbidden" food, what happens?

Let's talk about a nice, hot, gooey pizza--with extra cheese and whatever your favorite topping might be. You're at home, minding your business, sticking to your low-calorie (and low-interest, low-fun) diet, when suddenly you see an ad on TV for some delicious, satisfying pizza.

What do you do?

If you're like me (before I found the "Un-Diet"), once confronted with the intoxicating sight of that pizza, you suddenly find yourself in its power. The pizza becomes hypnotic, magical, sinful and captivating, an experience much like the on-the-wagon gambler who is suddenly faced with an unexpected casino slot machine!

God help anybody who's expecting you to make a nutritious, balanced dinner, because you're about` to order one of those yummy pizzas...and *eat four or five slices... before you know what's happened to you.*

In short, after depriving ourselves for even a short period of time, there is a subsequent tendency to overeat the forbidden food. The unfortunate fact is that after we deprive ourselves, on a psychological level we want that forbidden food even *more.* In addition, we are constantly bombarding ourselves and our loved ones with messages about "good" and "bad" foods. We even say things like "I was good today...I didn't eat anything bad".

"Good" food makes us feel like we've *been* good. "Bad" foods feel like they go directly to our hips and waistline--at least, that's what we've been conditioned to believe. So we stay away from those "bad" foods until one day, in a hungry and weak moment we cave in, eat way too much pizza, and then feel *really* bad.

I call this the Quiet Diet Riot--where our whole system goes insane and just has to eat all that bad, bad pizza until we're so overcome with guilt that we can barely look at our faces in the mirror...let alone our bodies. Deprivation leads to compulsive overeating...your body does the Quiet Diet Riot! And the Quiet Diet Riot leads to diet failure...and weight gain.

••

Deprivation leads to compulsive overeating...your body does the Quiet Diet Riot! And the Quiet Diet Riot leads to diet failure...and weight gain.

••

In this society, we're married to the idea that "bad" foods make you fat. For example, we really believe that fat makes us fat. So we eat lots and lots of fat-free foods. In fact, way too many fat-free foods. Actually, it is the avoidance of these "bad" foods that causes us to overeat them and subsequently gain weight! This is a profoundly simple truth, and one that chronic dieters find extremely difficult to accept. Yet anyone caught in the maze of diets needs desperately to grasp this key point-- avoiding "bad" foods causes us to overeat them and then gain weight. Remember the multi-billion dollar diet industry out there that depends on us thinking that there *are* forbidden foods, or foods that will definitely make us fat? That is how they coax us to spend our money on their books and products. We certainly can't trust ourselves, so we have to buy their program, or eat their food, or go to their meetings, or check in with their counselors.

If those programs did work, we would not need to do them again!...or do another program...or just get more self control! Dieting means that we must make certain foods "bad" and "forbidden"...which leads to deprivation...which leads to the Quiet Diet Riot...which leads to weight gain and depression. And once we get over the depression, what do we do? We find another diet...and start the whole unhappy cycle all over again!

Carol, 43, has always been stick-thin and never had to diet in her life to stay that way. It wasn't until she had a baby and gained weight that she went to her friends for help. Carol's (well-meaning) friends taught her how to diet. They told her she needed to start eating salads and stop eating fat. For the first time in her life, she became a dieter, and for the first time in her life, *she couldn't lose weight*. She came to see me. Two months after our work together, she said she felt better than she had in years, and that seven pounds had simply "fallen off" of her. I must confess that as her counselor I had some feelings of envy! While I was happy for her and certainly wanted her to have this result, I was also wondering how she learned in one weekend what took me a year to grasp!

Her answer was very clear. "The reason this was so easy for me," she explained, "is that this is how I always ate my whole life. It was only when I started dieting that I ceased to be able to maintain my natural tendency to be thin."

This made perfect sense to me, and I recalled Robert Schwartz's ground-breaking book, <u>Diets</u> <u>Don't</u> <u>Work</u> many years ago. He said that when they studied people who were trying to *gain* weight, they found that methods like milk shakes at bedtime, sundaes, excessive fat-filled desserts, etc., were all failing. Nothing worked, until they tried one last thing...*they put those people on a diet*! Only then were the subjects guaranteed a five-pound weight gain. They achieved that weight gain by having what you and I now recognize as a "Quiet Diet Riot." The only way for them to gain the needed weight was to go on a diet (and then blow the diet)! What does that tell <u>you</u>?

....

There are no forbidden foods. There are no *bad* foods. There are no foods that make us fat. All food is simply food...we attach judgments and significance to it!

....

We need to change the "connections" and belief systems about "forbidden" foods by establishing in our minds that *all foods are the same*. Does this mean that all foods serve us or honor us? NO. Does this mean that we will now eat key-lime pie for breakfast because food is food? No, we need to have some further knowledge of how certain foods SATIATE us and how to re-connect to our true sense of hunger. For now, I just want you to understand the significance of this deprivation mentality and its pervasiveness in our society.

Some of the most important studies along these lines are those of children and their reactions to so-called forbidden foods. In one study several eight-year-olds were placed in a room with several bowls filled with brightly-colored candy, including chocolate and other goodies. The children were told they could eat to their heart's content from any of the bowls, except for one bowl that was filled with small baby carrots. Researchers were amazed to see the immense proportion of carrots eaten to candy. Why did the kids eat the carrots and forgo the candy? Because they were told that carrots were a "forbidden food!"

This teaches a great deal about the psychological propensity to want what we can't have. The National Institute of Health has reviewed all published studies on the efficacy of weight-loss treatments, and found that "...interventions continue to produce short-term weight loss and long-term weight gain".[1] In addition, "For the vast majority, lost weight returns within months, and over time most dieters gain rather than lose weight".[2]

Some people think the tendency to eat in order to store fat is genetically based. And in one sense that's true. Some of your older relatives used to gorge themselves on fat whenever they got the chance. But not your great-grandparents. *Much* older relatives than that--I'm talking *cavemen!* The caveman would make a kill and then eat and store as much fat as he could. There was a simple reason for this...he never knew when he'd be able to make another killing, so eating a lot and storing fat was a

---

[1]   Heatherton TF, Mahamedi F, Striepe M, et al. A Ten-Year Longitudinal Study of Body Weight, Dieting, and Eating Disorder Symptoms. J Abnorm Psychol 1997; 106:117-1two5.

[2]   [National Task Force on the Prevention and Treatment of Obesity. Long-term pharmacotherapy in the management of obesity. JAMA 1997; two76:1907-1915.

necessity. Unfortunately, we still mimic this same pattern of eating too much--a pattern that's been handed down for thousands of years--even though we no longer have to *kill* for food, and despite the fact that there's a restaurant on every corner!

REASON #2 - WE'RE OUT OF TOUCH WITH OUR HUNGER

The second reason we're still gaining weight is that we are completely out of touch with our hunger, and are, therefore, eating too much.

We have much to learn from people who are naturally thin. When these people are asked "When do you eat?", their response is a slightly surprised, "When I'm hungry, of course!". Naturally-thin people hold many answers for us. Their experience teaches us that we need to adhere to their three basic concepts:

(1) They eat when they're hungry,
(2) They stop when they're satisfied (not full), and
(3) They taste and enjoy each bite. Basically, this is why thin people remain thin.

....

Eat when you're hungry, stop when you're satisfied (not full), and taste and enjoy each bite. Basically, this is why thin people remain thin.

....

Remember Chapter Two, the discussion of how an infant eats naturally, and how this changes as we get older? We've lost this ability to tune into our bodies for hunger signals.

We have been told that "Fat makes us fat," "Carbs make us fat," and "Protein makes us fat." In addition, many of us have read that "mixing certain foods together can cause rotting in the stomach." What's left? What are we supposed to eat? And if fat makes us fat, why are we more obese than ever, while, as a nation, we are eating less fat than ever before?! The grocery stores are jammed with fat-free foods that we're buying up like hotcakes.

What exactly is hunger? Why do we sometimes feel like we're hungry all day? Why, at other times, do we feel satisfied with less? How much of hunger is real hunger, and how much is emotional hunger?

First, a little explanation of why we get too hungry, why we overeat and why we feel so deprived:

The average working American awakens to either no breakfast or to a small non-nutritional pastry. With little or no fuel in the body, like a furnace without fuel to create heat/energy, the body cannot get started. Nothing prompts the body to heat up and start burning calories (start the metabolism). In contrast, with a morning meal, the body can heat up and burn off as much as two hundred to three hundred activity calories in a few hours.

After eating no breakfast at all, most people eat lunch when they're expected to do so, around noon. Once again, we get cut off from our feelings of hunger, eating instead in response to time on a clock. By this time, most people are *ravenous*. When we're this hungry, we tend to gravitate toward sugars (quick energy), and we tend to overeat. This, in turn, causes us to first, feel bad psychologically about our perceived indiscretion, and next to beat ourselves up, and believe we are bad, unworthy, or a failure. After this, there is a tendency to again say to ourselves, "Well, I just won't eat anymore today", so that again we repeat the process of starvation--overeat--feel bad, etc. We then have a tendency to focus all our attention on our weight, our food, and our obsession with our body, thus locking in emotional eating.

HOW DO WE GET BACK IN TOUCH WITH OUR HUNGER?

I'd like to offer you a simple, powerful tool for visualizing hunger and fullness. I call it "The Food/Fuel Tank." It will help you become re-connected to your body after years of being disconnected and giving your power to diets to tell you when to eat, what to eat, and when to stop eating. We can now take our power back by re-learning something we innately knew as a child...true hunger. Using this "The Food/Fuel Tank", we can have minute-by-minute results in knowing where we are in regard to our physical (not emotional) hunger.

E	1/4	1/2	3/4	F

The Food-Fuel Tank

E = Starving, dizzy, increased irritability, ravenous, empty

1/4 = Hungry, ready to eat

1/2 = Neither hungry nor full; comfortable

3/4 = Satisfied, no longer hungry

FULL = Stuffed, "Ate too much"

In order to begin re-connecting to your hunger, you must first re-learn when to eat and when to stop eating. We need to start eating when we go down as low as a quarter of a tank, which means "hungry, ready to eat." At that level, some people experience stomach growling, and others describe it as a slight tiredness. *Your* feelings at one-quarter are yours alone. The quarter-tank level comes *before* you start feeling irritable, which is when your stomach is on E for Empty.

A tip for re-learning how to get in touch with hunger: Start checking in with your food/fuel tank every 3-1/2 - 4 hours. This doesn't mean you should eat every 3-1/2 - 4 hours, however, because __that__ would not be eating in response to true hunger. It's more the fact that the body

needs to have feedings or refuelings approximately every 3-1/2 - 4 hours (when we are at one-quarter on the tank). And the rationale of using the word feeding rather than meal or snack is that all feedings are about the same size...approximately two fistfuls of food.

For most chronic dieters, this food/fuel tank will seem like learning a new language for quite a while, because we've put this intuition away for so many years. If we're too hungry between meals, we approach food differently. We can't be mindful when we're starving! Instead, we eat and eat to make sure we satisfy ourselves--thus overstuffing ourselves. Also, you might feel really odd and uncomfortable eating five to six feedings a day, rather than getting the "high" that comes from binging and starving on just two large meals a day. And that "high," along with habit, can be quite difficult to break.

The next step is to fill yourself with food, as slowly as you can, until you reach about 3/4 full, which means "satisfied, no longer hungry." *You no longer need to top off your tank to nourish yourself!*

Learning what 3/4 feels like can take some time. Most people will need to experience FULL several times before they get a real sense of "3/4-ness." Several clients have told me they have to get up to FULL for a while, and then say they work backward to about four less bites to experience a 3/4. Remember to be patient with this process of learning the Food/Fuel Tank. Even after years of doing this, I still sometimes find myself (usually while socializing) going past 3/4, to full.

This is what Candace, a physical therapist in her late twenties, told me: "At some point I figured out that I was definitely going to FULL, because I wasn't losing weight. However, I was creating thousands of stories before finally getting to 'Oh, yeah, I have to eat four less bites.'

"I was eating popcorn from those giant silver bowls while I watched TV. I called it three cups of popcorn, which equaled a bread exchange (a term left over from my dieting days). I'd sit and have that bowl of popcorn for dinner. You know how with popcorn you never get full? You get sick before you get full? I

34

would just find myself sick from the popcorn. When I finally got sick and tired of complaining about my weight, I knew I had to cut calories. For me, going from a FULL TANK to a 3/4 was like jumping off a cliff! Four less bites meant no more getting 'high' off food, no more drama around food, can't complain anymore about my weight. It took some getting used to, but it was worth it!" Natural body weight is the weight to which your body is naturally drawn, due to many factors. Your body reaches that weight when you are eating consciously, rather than dieting. It is different for everyone.

....

Natural body weight is the weight to which your body is naturally drawn, due to many factors. Your body reaches that weight when you are eating consciously, rather than dieting. It is different for everyone.

....

Some of the factors that influence your natural body weight are genetics, age, life stressors, etc. Does this mean we are doomed to be like our relatives? Yes, in some ways, and No in most ways. *We do not have to be overweight, and we can absolutely be fit at any size.*

The Food/Fuel Tank is something you will have to practice and experience for some time before it feels comfortable. Some of my clients report that it took as much as an entire year to get comfortable with the Tank. Remember that we're not putting you on a diet! You're going on the Un-Diet, which actually requires a different mind-set from any diet you've done before. We're not just changing a few items on your menu or declaring a few things off-limits. Quite the contrary! We're actually empowering you to eat what you want...when you are *physically* hungry. We know this takes a giant leap of faith, and that this change of thinking won't come overnight. It will be well worth the time and effort when you can feel empowered around food, rather than victimized by it.

Keep in mind also that the Tank is not an absolute. It's a rough--but fairly accurate--guide to eating. In fact, none of the information in the field of nutrition is absolute. We make educated judgments, based on facts, which can be debated incessantly. We simply present methods for maintaining weight that are consistent with the way the body naturally seeks to be. The reason this can take so long, however, is that most of us have been out of touch with our physical hunger for years, if not our entire life. Be patient with the process.

Here are some reasons why we tend to go over the 3/4 level:

1. Quiet Diet Riot: You've been depriving yourself; you've been good, you deserve a treat. You're hungry, you're tired, you're weak, you overeat.

2. Emotional reasons: If you are faced with fear, worry, anger, sadness, boredom, confrontation, turbulence, or relationship difficulties, or even positive emotions like celebration and joy, it is common to turn to eating, subconsciously seeking to avoid the threatening emotions, confrontations, or perceived expectations.

3. Lack of Education About Eating: If you don't understand the concept of satiation, or which foods will keep you satisfied over longer periods of time and not burn off so quickly (see Chapter Four), you will tend to go over 3/4.

4. Getting too hungry, or allowing yourself to move to E on the Tank often causes people to go over a 3/4.

Understand that excessive use of alcohol and/or drugs is a saboteur of any program of conscious eating, by virtue of the fact that it takes us out of consciousness. Remember, the stomach naturally holds about three to four hours worth of food, also called glucose, or fuel. Therefore, a good way to determine if you got to 3/4 is that in three to four hours you will again be a 1/4, comfortably hungry. If you are not hungry in three or four hours, you either: (1) overate at the previous feeding, or (2) you are perhaps still so out of touch that you don't yet know when you're hungry. Don't feel bad if that's the case. It's quite normal.

Bottom line on weight loss and eating: If you get up to FULL, or stuffed, two or more times a week, you will probably gain weight, because you will have accumulated, over time, the surplus of calories (3500 above your BMR; as explained in the next chapter) that causes weight gain. If you get to 3/4's consistently, you will probably lose weight, if you are not already at your natural body weight, and you will probably maintain your weight if you are already at your natural body weight. If you only get to 1/2, that means in about an hour you will be hungry and ready to eat again, which can easily result in overeating.

HOW BIG IS YOUR STOMACH?

Another way to understand what a 3/4 feels like is to *imagine the actual size of the stomach.... it's about the size of a medium baked potato. It holds approximately two handfuls of food per feeding. Thus, we want to eat approximately two handfuls of food per feeding.*

Some examples of a handful would be:

Small baked potato

4 oz. piece of fish, chicken, meat

Piece of fruit

Regular size sandwich

Two or three cookies
A cup or so of regular or frozen yogurt

Small piece of cheesecake

Measuring cup of rice, beans, or pasta

(Please remember that these are intended to be rough measurements because every body is different.)

Here's an idea of how you can visualize a body efficiently taking in and expending calories: in general, the average female body (with an average amount of physical workouts), burns approximately 100-120 calories per hour. The stomach *holds* approximately three to four hours' worth of food. Therefore, if the average female were to eat approximately 400 calories per feeding, her body could efficiently take in and then burn off each feeding, thus allowing her body to stay lean and trim. Remember, this is only an approximation. Please understand that there will be feedings where you will exceed this amount, and some where you will be under. *We do not advocate chronic calorie counting.* Instead, we feel it much more important to learn and follow the Food/Fuel Tank. It's too difficult to count, and so much more freeing to allow our body to dictate our needs.

What about alcohol? Can we have a glass of wine with dinner? The whole idea is to cease the deprivation mentality, so that food and eating takes on a completely new feel for you. Have a glass of wine as one handful; and have a piece of fish or chicken, for example, as a second handful, to satiate yourself. Does two handfuls mean I can have two drinks?! No, for numerous reasons. First, there's no experience of satiation with two drinks. Second, you'll be starving at the same time as losing your inhibitions...and you'll overeat...big time! Third, when we let ourselves go out of consciousness, our eating also becomes unconscious ...the exact opposite of Un-Dieting. Check it out for yourself which foods satiate you. That's more valuable than taking my word for it anyway. When you do, however, have your moments of unconsciousness and unconscious eating, forgive yourself for being human, and simply pick this back up at your next meal. No Beating Yourself Up!

To sum up, in order to get back in touch with our real hunger, we must learn to check in with our Food/Fuel Tank, every three and one-half to four hours, and honor the body's innate wisdom to seek refueling, rather than forcing it to wait until a more convenient time to eat.

REASON THREE: EMOTIONAL EATING

The third reason America's gaining more and more weight, along with the Quiet Diet Riot and being out of touch with our hunger, is what I call "emotional eating."

Emotional eating, simply stated, is eating because of something other than hunger. We do it because we're out of touch with our physiological hunger, and instead hungry over unmet emotional needs. Here are the most common emotional reasons why people eat: anger, sadness, fear, loneliness, worry, elation, fatigue, hunger for love, hunger for attention, frustration, embarrassment, upset, discomfort, avoidance, uneasiness, conflict, depression, anxiousness, pain, grief, longing, boredom, lust, unfulfilled expectations, unmet goals, feelings of failure, feelings of impending doom, and joy.

Emotional eating also occurs if we don't feel effective at communicating our needs and getting them met. It can be because we don't know how to say "no" to people. We may take on too much in our lives, just to please (or appease) other people, and it can come from not telling our spouses what we want from them.

Many times we eat out of habit, i.e., having popcorn at the movies. For some people, this is so automatic that they never even question whether or not they're hungry...we're at the movies, of course we'll have popcorn! For others, talking on the phone or watching television or reading the newspaper are instant signals to start snacking. Much of this type of eating is unconscious, and many times we don't even realize how much we've eaten until we feel full, tired or sick.

I must confess that I've often caught myself eating out of what I thought was boredom. What we call boredom, though, is usually an avoidance of other emotions. I saw that my eating was really more of an excuse to take a break. I often need breaks--we all do. But I tend to find myself, as do many of my clients, feeling that I must be productive at all times. Very often our identity is associated with being productive; so if we're not productive, we feel lost. What are we going to be praised for if we're not running around and doing things? What would people think if we just sat there, doing nothing? What would I think of myself if I just sat there? What kind of feelings might come up that I might not be able to handle? Sometimes these new thoughts are scary.

This is from my colleague and friend Diana:

"I remember being four years old, sitting in the bathroom with my brother and sister, when we got a phone call from my dad telling us that mom had died. I can even remember where each one of us was sitting in that bathroom. My brother and sister were crying. I didn't understand. In that moment, I somehow felt the need to take care of the two of them so that they wouldn't leave me. This was simply how my four-year-old mind worked. I made an emotional decision that I'd better take care of people so they wouldn't leave me.

"In the next week after my mom's death, I remember being very confused because nobody explained to me what had happened. Looking back, perhaps they did, but I didn't understand. All these people came over to our house, and everyone brought food for us to eat. I remember two things: confusion and eating a lot, until I was very full. And for some reason I looked forward to seeing what food was left over whenever people left the house. This became a "connection" for me...confusion leads to food.

"I did that in college, too. Whenever I got confused with homework, or was feeling abandoned, I went to the familiar memory that food was comfort."

For Diana, at age four, two very consequential connections were made:

(1) You better take care of people (be a good little girl), and
(2) When you're confused, go eat.

....

Emotional eating can be triggered by events that happened long ago.

....

Can you see how we learn to eat out of feelings other than hunger? It is imperative that we take a look at all the emotional reasons we eat, so that we can become once again, tuned into our own bodies, as we were in infancy. Taking a look at our emotional eating can easily be the hardest part of reading this book. It will always be difficult, as we revisit this self-exploration throughout our life.....but it's well worth the effort.

We may also eat out of fear of change. Can you imagine all the changes there would be in your life if you were to lose your weight? There would be new expectations, new relationships, new feelings with old relationships, new challenges, new fears, new confrontations, new clothes, new conversations, new you. And what if you don't like the new you?! (We hear this particular fear quite often). There would be a whole different set of conversations going on in your head. Think about how much time you spend right now obsessing about food! What would you replace all that chatter with? What would it be like to no longer have excuses in your head for why you do or don't do things? What would you now be expected to do? How would you be expected to be?

Mike, 41, is an air traffic controller. Here's what he told me after six sessions:

"I was afraid that if I was too thin, I wouldn't be safe. My extra twenty pounds were like a safety shield between me and the rest of the world. Also, if I were thin, women would like me, and then I'd have to deal with that whole thing. Keeping that extra fat on my body was my way of telling women, "Keep away. There's no room for you here."

Sound familiar? Do you have any idea how many people are distressed with and plagued by fears?! Fear is something that is usually learned early in life, and it snowballs and solidifies later in life, until and unless a person can break free from its effects. It is certainly a typical reason that provokes people to eat. Emotional eating keeps us stuck in, and focused on, our fear.

Also involved with emotional eating is our need to suffer and drag drama into our lives...mostly to make our lives more colorful and interesting. Suffering and drama is very much learned behavior. If you come from a home where mom or dad was a drama queen or king, you learned how to suffer. It is sometimes extremely difficult to un-learn something like that. One of my clients is a woman in her 50's who came to me because her eating and weight were out of control. In exploring her life, she told me she has been in college for the last eighteen years, taking undergraduate and graduate courses, without the need to attain a specific degree. Every time she would come to see me, she would literally drag herself into my office, and I knew she could hardly wait to tell me how hard it all was for her...working full time and then attending school too.

One day, I challenged her need to drag herself around with the school thing, and I said, "Since you apparently love school...you've been going for eighteen years...would you be willing to believe, from now on, that school is effortless?"

She was flabbergasted by the question, because she truly felt that school was hard and difficult. She did not understand that she was choosing to view school as hard and difficult, and so it was. Whatever you call something is what it will be for you. I suggested that she start changing the language she used so that she'd say, "School is effortless, and I love learning." She did so--and in the process, she realized that she had always thought of her life as a burden...her whole life. It was something her mother always did, and thus, what she learned. And when she was suffering like this, it was a reason to turn to food.

Her connection became drama, oh, I'll eat. Because she was willing to change her thinking and her language, she says it became much more fun and rewarding to go to school. In addition, she made a decision to complete a Master's Degree in Education, which is a remarkable achievement for anyone. She is also doing much less emotional eating, and her weight is dropping naturally.

Here's a way to start your exploration:

EXERCISE:

Which emotional issues or feelings are so hard for me that I drift toward food and eating, rather than dealing with them?

_____

_____

_____

_____

_____

_____

_____

Would I be willing to deal with these issues, so that they no longer trigger emotional eating?

Write "yes" or "no" by each issue. We'll return to this list later on, so hang on to it...just a little longer.

REASON #4 - WE HAVE INACCURATE INFORMATION

Okay. Let's review. The first three reasons why America's gaining weight are: (1) Quiet Diet Riot, (2) We're Out of Touch With Our Hunger; (3) We're Eating Our Emotions, and now reason number (4): We're getting faulty information about diets and food.

With so much information out there, it is surprising we could be uneducated. Unfortunately, we are being grossly misinformed by the media and others professing to be "nutrition experts", usually so that they can sell some expensive new product or gimmicky diet. Eight hundred *billion* dollars are spent annually on health care! The American public has become consumed with fitness and weight loss. So we have become easy targets for unscrupulous people and multi-million-dollar corporations who know that the typical American wants a pain-free, quick solution to weight loss. In addition, we have slowly and methodically been brainwashed to believe that we will have everything we ever wanted as soon as we are thin. Television commercials and magazine ads subliminally and overtly exhibit the haggard single woman whose life is in total disarray until she finds the little weight-loss pill that allows her to acquire the husband, house and life of her dreams.

Why are we so easily manipulated? Because we have a quick-fix mentality, where we believe everything can and should be easy and painless. We want to believe that a pill can burn up all the extra calories we ingest as a result of not facing up to our out-of-control and dishonest lives. We don't want the job of having to take action to fix the problems in our lives. And we certainly don't want to suffer in any way by having to restrict ourselves from having what we want. We would much rather have a magic pill or a surgeon who will *cut* the fat away.

Following are the ten most common myths about food, dieting and weight loss:

1) MYTH: Fat makes you fat.

FACT: AMERICANS ARE MORE OBESE TODAY THAN EVER BEFORE IN HISTORY, AND WE ARE EATING MORE FAT-FREE THAN EVER! Can you see that fat isn't the thing that's making us fat?!

The only way a human being can gain a pound of fat in one day (aside from a metabolic disorder and/or genetics) is by eating 3,500 calories above our basal metabolic rate, as explained in the next chapter. This is 3,500 calories above what you need to efficiently run your body. Not a hundred calories, not five hundred, but *three thousand, five hundred calories.* that's a lot of calories! It's actually quite difficult to eat that many calories. It is *irrelevant* whether the calories comes from protein, carbohydrate or fat. It can be 3,500 calories from pure protein, pure carbohydrate or pure fat. We'll get more technical about this later on, but eating fat doesn't make you fat. For now, keep in mind that only by eating 3,500 extra calories above and beyond BMR--from any source--can we gain an extra pound of fat.

2) MYTH: We gain weight, food rots in the stomach and we become "toxic" if we combine foods improperly, i.e.,

44

eat carbohydrate and protein together. Blending certain foods together can cause rotting in the stomach and weight gain.

FACT: The human body has three different metabolic pathways that release different digestive enzymes, so that all food is digested. The whole food blending business is unscientific. The only part of food that isn't digested is fiber, and this is excreted into the colon and eliminated. It doesn't matter which foods you eat together, because all food is digested, and nothing rots in the stomach. We need to remember how magnificently the body is designed, and that any food not digested is excreted through the colon.

So it's not combinations of food that put fat on you. It's overeating.

3) MYTH: Our stomach gets stretched out when we overeat, and shrinks when we eat less.

FACT: The stomach expands when food is ingested, but once digested, the stomach returns to the same size. Grossly overweight people have stomachs pretty much the same size as those of thin people--they're generally about the size of two handfuls of food, or a medium-sized baked potato. When you lose weight, your stomach doesn't "shrink" or get smaller. Instead, you lose pockets of fat *around* the stomach. The stomach doesn't put on weight when you do. People might have big bellies--but not big stomachs.

We may *believe* our stomachs shrink when we diet because when we are eating consciously, the amount of food needed for satiation is less. So when we eat less, the stomach expands less. But it doesn't get heavier or lighter--we do.

4) MYTH: If you eat after six or seven p.m., you will gain weight.

FACT: Again, the only way to gain one pound of fat is by eating 3,500 calories above your basal metabolic rate. If you have not eaten that extra 3,500 calories, how can the food eaten late at night be singled out for putting fat on your body? It doesn't matter what time we overeat. Too many calories equals excess weight, period, end of story.

5) MYTH: Vitamins and mineral supplements will give your body more energy.

FACT: The only thing that gives us sustained energy is a Calorie. Calories are only found in food, and small quantities in select herbs. Since vitamins and mineral supplements do not contain calories, they cannot give us energy. They may provide nutrients missing in our diets, such as, for example, calcium to prevent osteoporosis or iron for anemia. This should be determined by a physician and/or a registered dietitian performing a dietary analysis.

6) MYTH: Sugar and carbohydrates make you gain weight.

FACT: Again, *only if your overall calorie intake exceeds your needs by 3,500 calories.* But sugar and carbohydrates *do burn off as energy very quickly, thus causing us to become hungry again sooner.* This leads to eating more and increased caloric consumption. If you eat sugar and carbohydrates with a little protein or fat, the latter will help buffer the carbohydrate from burning off as quickly, and will thus keep you satiated for a longer (three to four hour) period of time.

7) MYTH: If you eat breakfast, you will remain hungrier all day long because now your body is *expecting* more food.

FACT: The body is already expecting food. It works much like a furnace. If you feed it fuel (food) in the morning, it starts heating up and burning calories. This is exactly what you want it to do. So, by not eating until noon, your body can't get started, and it can't burn the two hundred to three hundred calories it normally burns when you eat first thing. The reason you may feel hungrier all day after eating breakfast is because the body is efficiently burning calories, the very thing needed for weight loss. <u>Losing weight isn't about eating less! It's about eating mindfully...and more often, so that the total calories consumed is less</u>.

....

Losing weight isn't about eating less! It's about eating mindfully...and more often, so that the total calories consumed is less.

....

8) MYTH: Vegetables are a "free food". You can eat unlimited quantities without weight gain.

FACT: While vegetables are low in calories and do not have fat, they still contain calories. Because people think vegetables are a "free" food, they tend to binge on them. Since they have a low satiety level, which leads to eating more, we are back to excess calorie consumption, which is the way to gain weight. The most common food in this category is baby carrots. Many people use these for what we call "unconscious munching", meaning munching while watching television, while on the telephone, while driving, etc. While they may look harmless, an average bag contains approximately six hundred calories! And did you ever hear anyone say, after eating a whole bag of baby carrots, "Wow that was great...now I'm satisfied!"? So, since we're not satisfied, we end up eating more and/or switching to another food for satiation. Then we wonder why we've gained weight... after all, it was just carrots!

9) MYTH: Fast food is bad for you.

FACT: Because of the increased attention to health and weight, fast food restaurants have been forced to decrease fat content and switch to unsaturated fats for cooking. They have better salad bars and usually have "heart-smart" meals available, sometimes even offering separate menus for the health-conscious. What we need to move toward now is getting restaurants to decrease their portions, which would greatly help in weight management. Since that's probably not going to happen in this lifetime (mainly because so many people deprive themselves, then want those big portions), the best you can do is wrap up half your meal and take it with you for a later feeding. This is also an excellent psychological move, since wrapping up food for later gives you a great reminder that there is always more food, and you won't get hungry.

10) MYTH: Restricting certain foods, such as desserts and alcohol, will help you lose weight.

FACT: This is probably the number one reason why people do not lose weight, and in fact, gain weight! It is what we have termed Quiet Diet Riot, the result of food restriction. Remember, when we restrict our favorite foods, like chocolate-chip cookies or double cheese pizza, we count on our will power to control our desire. This usually works pretty well....for a while. When we are subsequently placed in a situation with the forbidden or "bad" food and perhaps a bit too much hunger, we may subconsciously feel we'll never have the opportunity again; so we eat the whole plate, saying we will "start our diet tomorrow", thus consuming too many calories and gaining weight. The weight gain, remember, is not from the "bad" food, but from the excess calories.

Fraudulent weight-loss products and programs often rely on persuasive combinations of mystique, obscure ingredients and messages that "sound reasonable," such as fat-burning pills. A weight-loss program may be fraudulent if one or more of the following are true:

-- It claims or implies a large or fast weight-loss, using words such as "easy", "effortless", "guaranteed" or "permanent"
-- It requires special foods purchased from the company rather than conventional stores
-- It implies weight loss without restricting calories or exercising, and discounts the benefits of exercise
-- It uses terms such as: miraculous, breakthrough, exclusive, secret, unique, ancient, accidental discovery, or doctor-developed
-- Claims to get rid of "cellulite"
-- Relies heavily on undocumented case histories, before and after photos, and testimonials by "satisfied customers" (who are often paid for testimony written by the advertiser)
-- Misuses medical or technical terms, claims government approval
-- Professes to be a treatment for a wide range of ailments and nutritional deficiencies, as well as for weight loss
-- Promotes a medically-unsupervised diet of less than 1000 calories per day
-- Fails to state risks or recommend a medical exam
-- Gives mystical properties to certain foods or ingredients
-- Uses high-pressure tactics, such as one-time-only deals or pyramid-type sales
-- Promotes a nutritional plan without relying on at least one author or counselor with nutrition credentials (registered dietitians and nutrition educators are preferred)

Now you know the four reasons why we as a nation are more obese than ever:

(1) Quiet Diet Riot, (2) We're out of touch with our hunger, (3) We are doing "Emotional Eating" and (4) We have inaccurate information ...we're being brainwashed by the media.[3]

In the next chapter, you'll learn the true key to weight loss, something that diet hucksters with something to sell you would never reveal.

[3]   Berg, Weight Loss Fraud and Quackery. Healthy Weight Journal/Obesity and Health 1990; 4:9:71 Calorie Control Council; 1998 Food and Drug Administration; 1998 National Association to Advance Fat Acceptance; 1998 Creatine, Karen, "Moving Beyond Diets", Largesse, the Network for Size Esteem, 1998 Mayo Foundation for Medical Education and Research; 1998

Chapter Four -- Satiation: Are You Getting Enough?

In this chapter, I'm going to give you the key to Un-Dieting...the approach to eating that will get you to your ideal weight *without* dieting, *without* forbidden foods, and *without* special meals for which you have to pay a diet company thousands of dollars a year. Reading this chapter can change the way you approach food forever. Before we talk about getting to your natural body weight, let's make sure we understand exactly what it means...to gain weight.

Here's what Diana has to say about fat:

"I believed when I ate fat that I could physically FEEL fat growing on my leg! I felt fat, so no matter what weight I was, I still *felt* fat. I never lost weight by cutting fat from my diet, but I felt better in my head. So my head determined whether I was thin or fat!

"I ate lots of fat-free food, and never lost weight; so I thought, 'Well, I guess I have to restrict more fat.' The more I restricted fat, the more calories I consumed, not realizing I was eating more. Then, feeling so restricted, I ate a cookie, and as soon as I did, I returned to feeling like the Goodyear blimp. I was convinced once again that it was the fat in the cookie that was making me gain weight!"

Diana came to realize that her feelings about fat did not reflect *medical* fat. Let's look at exactly what goes on as fat is formed in the body.

When you "feel fat growing on your body," what's really happening is that you are disassociating from your feelings and projecting them onto your body. Disassociating can be described as **the mind's way of taking your thoughts to your body, so that you won't have to feel the more intense pain of the emotional issues you're not facing**. Another way to look at it: it's your *mind's habitual* desire to keep you from dealing with stuff that feels scary and/or threatening. *Any* time you *feel* fat, it's always disassociation. It is what Dana Armstrong, R.D., Jane

Hirschmann and Carol Munter, in their book *Intuitive Eating,* call the *"Anatomy of a Fat Thought."*

It is therefore, important that you take the time to understand how fat is REALLY formed on the body.

The human body burns calories (energy) in two ways. The first way is through our involuntary activities, such as the beating of the heart, the inhaling of oxygen, and maintenance of body temperature. The second is through our voluntary activities, such as exercising and moving around throughout our day.

Most of us already understand the burning of calories during physical activity, but we don't realize that we expend a great deal of energy on the *involuntary* process, also known as Basal Metabolic Rate (BMR). The BMR is the rate at which calories are expended when our body is at rest, just for our bodily functions to take place. BMR is surprisingly high. A woman whose total energy needs are 2,000 calories a day may spend more than half of these, as much as 1200-1400 calories, simply maintaining her BMR processes, without moving from her chair!

People often don't realize that so much of their energy is going to support this basic work of the body. *These BMR minimum energy needs must be met first, before any calories can be used toward physical activity.* This means that we must have food in the body (calories/energy) in order for these involuntary actions to take place. Therefore, if we are *not* feeding ourselves properly, the body, an *extremely* smart machine, must go somewhere else to get the energy (or calories) it needs.

Where does it go? It can go to muscle. When the body depletes the muscle, we are creating the exact opposite of what we want, because *muscle burns calories.* So we are robbing ourselves of our best calorie-burner. The body is not only smart, but in these actions, it is seeking to keep us alive by going to these places to get calories.

BMR is different for each person and is influenced by several things. Younger people can have a higher metabolic rate, usually because of increased weight-bearing activities. Height also affects BMR. Taller people will generally have increased metabolic rate due to a greater skin surface from which heat is lost. Third, gender influences BMR. Males generally have faster metabolisms than females, due to the greater percentage of lean tissue in the male body. Lastly, muscle tissue is the largest determinant of calorie-burning, which means that building muscle is a great way to burn more calories.

Fasting and malnutrition <u>lower</u> the BMR, because of the loss of lean tissue...the exact opposite of what a dieter is trying to do. Instead of encouraging the body to run well and burn calories properly, dieting *inhibits* your body from awakening and burning the energy/calories you want it to burn.

Let's look at the practical implications of this. I used to feel lucky that I wasn't hungry in the morning. I was secretly excited that I could prolong eating until noon, sometimes up to two p.m.! I sheepishly mentioned this to Diana, who proceeded to enlighten me about what I was *really* doing. She explained that by starving my body of the fuel it needed to start burning calories first thing in the morning, I was ripping myself off from burning up to 1,300 calories! Instead, my body, sensing starvation and being the brilliant machine it is, went to my muscles for energy (calories). Therefore, in addition to losing the opportunity to burn over a thousand calories, my exercise and weight training was being sabotaged.

Many of our clients respond to this fearfully, saying, "But if I eat first thing in the morning, I stay hungry all day!" What is really happening is that your body is *efficiently* burning off the food and naturally wants more feedings approximately every three to four hours if you are following the hunger scale and satiation concepts. Put another way, you are efficiently eating and burning off your feedings, thus maintaining your weight and/or losing weight.

BMR can be calculated, if you desire, by a registered dietitian and/or an exercise physiologist. For those who would prefer to use an *average* figure, Diana has found, after 14 years experience calculating BMR, the average female's BMR to be 1300-1400 calories. The average male is 1800-2000 calories, mainly because of differences in height, weight and lean tissue.

As mentioned earlier, the only way a human being can gain 1 pound of fat (aside from a metabolic disorder and/or genetics) is by eating 3500 calories over and above his or her Basal Metabolic Rate (BMR). It is irrelevant whether the calories come from protein, carbohydrate or fat. Many times, the morning after a big meal or a binge-eating experience, women will get on the scale, expecting that they've put on a few pounds. Let's see scientifically what you'd have to eat in order to gain a pound of fat in one day.

A woman's average BMR is 1300 calories, which means a woman burns 1300 calories a day just through involuntary activities (heart beating, digestive system, etc.). A woman would typically burn another four hundred calories from thirty to sixty minutes of any cardiovascular activities.

Remember that a pound of fat comes from eating 3500 extra calories above this BMR. Add 3500 calories to the 1700 you'll burn normally in one day...and you'll see that you'd have to eat a whopping 5200 calories *in one day* to put on just one extra pound of fat! I don't care how many chocolate chip cookies you eat, it would be very difficult to eat this many calories. Ditto for pizza, M&Ms, or whatever your particular indulgence may be.

The trouble comes when we *spread those 3500 calories out over time--let's say, a week.* It isn't that difficult to eat 500 extra calories a day, which would total 3500 calories over a week...and there's that extra pound of fat. But the key lesson of Un-Dieting is this:

REAL WEIGHT GAIN COMES FROM THE CONSUMPTION OF AN EXCESS AMOUNT OF CALORIES GENERALLY RESULTING FROM THE *DEPRIVATION* OF FOODS AND NOT BEING *MINDFUL* ABOUT HUNGER, SATIATION, AND EMOTIONAL EATING.

....

REAL WEIGHT GAIN COMES FROM THE CONSUMPTION OF AN EXCESS AMOUNT OF CALORIES GENERALLY RESULTING FROM THE *DEPRIVATION* OF FOODS AND NOT BEING *MINDFUL* ABOUT HUNGER, SATIATION, AND EMOTIONAL EATING.

....

It's not those so-called forbidden foods that make people fat. It's the idea of depriving ourselves of what we truly want...only to set up a binge-fest down the road. If you keep in mind the concepts of Un-Dieting, you'll never have to count another calorie...or go on another diet...or eat self-destructively...ever again! So let's now turn to the concept of *satiation*, so that you can enjoy the benefits of Un-Dieting for yourself.

Diana has this to say: "Most of my life growing up, I never knew what a calorie was, even though it was on every food package around. All I seemed to absorb from the media was a fear of fat. This preoccupation with fat kept me from seeing the truth about calories and consumption."

I would like to give you the basics of food and satisfaction that I feel you need to know to succeed.

A calorie is a source of heat that gives the body energy. It is the only substance on earth that can give a body energy. As we just saw, it is a fallacy that vitamin and mineral supplements give the body energy. They don't have calories. There are three types of calories:

1. Carbohydrate
2. Protein
3. Fat

Let's look at *Carbs* first. There are two types of carbs, simple and complex. Simple carbs are foods like sugar, syrup, honey, hard candy, etc., almost like saying "simply" sugar. Complex carbohydrates are foods like pasta, rice, cereal, bread, potatoes, fruit, and vegetables.

Protein: There are two types, animal protein and vegetable protein. Examples of vegetable protein are tofu and seitan. Animal protein is chicken, fish, turkey, meat (beef), pork, and eggs (only the whites). Legumes and beans are 70% carbohydrate and 30% protein.

Fat: These are foods such as butter, margarine, oil, mayo, salad dressing, fat on meats, etc.

We have a tendency to choose carbs over protein, because carbs send a chemical called serotonin to the brain, which has a calming effect. A high-carb diet is quick fuel. Lots of us think we're addicted to carbs, especially simple carbs (sugar)--and that our "carbohydrate addiction" is proof that our bodies are out of whack. Guess what--everyone is addicted to carbs! That's because carbs make us feel good. It's not unhealthy--it's just a simple fact. Carbs are a healthy part of anybody's diet.

Of the three nutrients, carbs, protein, and fat, we find that carbohydrates break down the fastest into glucose (sugar), thus peaking our blood sugars quickly. This feels good. Unfortunately, our blood sugars then drop off very quickly, leading us to be hungry again quicker. We then eat more food, or calories. THIS leads us to the extra 3500 calories to form one pound of fat on the body. Since protein breaks down more slowly and actually forms a buffer for the carbohydrates, it is wise to have some protein with your carbohydrates, so it will carry your fullness, or satiety, over a longer period of time. This will ultimately have us consuming less calories. The protein will satiate you until your next feeding.

....

Since protein breaks down more slowly and actually forms a buffer for the carbohydrates, it is wise to have some protein with your carbohydrates, so it will carry your fullness, or satiety, over a longer period of time. This will ultimately have us consuming less calories. The protein will help to satiate you until your next feeding.

....

For example, when having a bowl of pasta (carbs), add a small chicken breast (protein) to satiate you longer. I have learned to love egg whites on top of pasta marinara. If you're having a salad, add some turkey, tuna fish, or egg. Some diets tell you not to eat bread. On the Un-Diet, as we've said, there are no forbidden foods. So enjoy bread, and feel free to enjoy sandwiches. Be sure to include protein, such as turkey, tuna, or chicken.

We do need to be mindful of getting good value for our calorie money. This means understanding which foods break down more slowly, thus keeping you satisfied for the least amount of calories. If you're going to "spend" calories on a meal, get the most fullness/satiation value for the buck! It's up to you to experiment and find out what foods satiate you...and for how long. Everybody's different. For example, I eat a baked potato and feel perfectly content and satiated for two to two and a half hours. Baked potatoes don't create that much satiation time for my husband, however. Also, for me, if I know that dinner is an hour and a half away, but I'm already starting to get hungry, one protein bar will satiate me for that whole time, so that I won't have to approach my dinner starving. Food satiation is different for everyone--so you'll need to see for yourself which foods satiate you, and for how long. I think you'll actually enjoy the process.

When we talk about "spending" calories to maximize value, the obvious metaphor is spending money. Let me give you an example. I once left my dentist to go to another one, who promised to give me a better price on a couple of crowns. The job ended up being extremely painful, I was uncomfortable in his office, didn't like his staff, had to incur more visits, thus more time from work, and it really ended up costing me much more than if I had gone with my original dentist.

Just as we often pay more money to get less, we sometimes use our calorie money in an equally unwise manner. Let's take an example. One-half cup (or three spoonfuls) of pasta, cereal or rice contain one hundred calories. So does a baked potato. All are carbs, but which, for the same one hundred calories, do you think would leave you feeling full for a longer period of time? If you already have some mindfulness about eating, you would choose the baked potato. A potato would take you to a 3/4 on the Food/Fuel Tank. Do you think you would get to a 3/4 with *three spoonfuls of pasta*?!

Protein is a buffer for the carbs, because it burns off more slowly. That's how protein satiates us and thus carries us through to our next feeding. You don't have to count calories or grams of fat/carbs/protein on the Un-Diet. All you have to do is be roughly aware that you're not eating all carbs all the time, and buffer those carbs with protein to satiate. That's the freedom of the "Un-Diet"!

Protein is a buffer for the carbs, because it burns off more slowly. That's how protein satiates us and thus carries us through to our next feeding.

Fat takes the longest of the three nutrients to break down into glucose (sugar), which means it does keep us satisfied over a longer period of time. Ever notice after a high-fat Thanksgiving meal how you feel full for a while, and lose your energy? That's because fat doesn't burn off quickly. So, is fat bad for you? Does fat make you fat? No, it doesn't! Too much fat, however, *can* cause cardiovascular disease. That's why it needs to be consumed in moderation, especially when your genetics indicate a history of cardiovascular disease. Genetics aside, the American Heart Association says that 20% of our calories can come from fat, without creating risk for heart disease.

The great news for "Un-Dieters" is this: even if you could eat all the fat you wanted, you would never want to eat an amount of fat that would put your health at risk. Your body *intuitively* knows how much fat it wants. Too much fat makes us feel tired, can cause indigestion, and makes us lethargic. If you want to know how much fat to consume, ask the only diet doctor that counts--your own body!!!

Protein, added to carbs, increases your sense of satiation. You'll feel full on fewer calories...so you won't need to "binge eat" an hour later!

Now you know the simple secret of how weight is gained and lost. It all comes down to eating too many calories in the course of a day, a week, a month, a lifetime. Satiation--feeling full--offers the key to saying "Enough, thanks. My Food/Fuel Tank's already at 3/4...and I'm not going to *need* to eat for another three to four hours." Of course, if you want a cookie...or a few cookies...prior to your next real meal, hey, enjoy! Since you're listening to your body, you'll know when you've had enough.

Most diets that you see advertised on TV or read about in diet books are like amateur detectives, hot on the trail of the mysterious and evil food that makes us fat. The Fattening Food is out there somewhere, and diet authors are going to blow its cover! The problem is that all those well-meaning books come to completely opposite--and confusing--conclusions.

Some diet books tell you not to eat protein. Others tell you to cut down your carbs. Still others blame calories derived from fat. In other words, everybody's got to have a villain, a bad guy, some kind of food to blame.

Not the Un-Diet. Blaming a kind of food leads to *deprivation* and not taking responsibility for your food choices. And deprivation triggers binge eating of that food! So let's put away our magnifying glasses and flashlights. The search for Bad Food is over--because there's no such thing as a bad food. Carbs aren't the problem. Fat isn't the problem. Protein isn't the problem. Looking for a villain...a bad food...now, *that's* the real problem!

Let's take a quick look at how this plays out for us on a psychological level. When we're overweight, we're generally *angry* about it. Since we don't want to be angry at ourselves (that's no fun!), we engage in a search for villains. We want to find something other than ourselves to blame. That way, we don't have to take responsibility for our own eating. If we're blaming a kind of food, we're alleviating our own guilt over being overweight. Unfortunately, the strategy fails, because villainizing a type of food triggers deprivation, which triggers the big binge down the road. So let's stop blaming anything or anyone. There is no bad guy here. Let's take a more productive approach to our eating...and watch the pounds melt away.

A word about exercise. And that word is...*"essential."* Exercise simply *has* to be a commitment you make for the rest of your life. But I want you to make one vital shift in the way you think about working out, training, running, or whatever you like to do. Don't view it as "I've *got* to go exercise," because that's doomed to failure. That smacks of victimhood or even martyrdom. Instead, tell yourself, "I *get* to do this.. for *myself*."

My colleague Diana tells the story of how she was speaking with a client, complaining to that client that she had to go work out. Diana had forgotten for that one moment that this long-time client was in a wheelchair. The client sweetly reminded her, and added, "Ya know, Diana, I'd give everything I own to get out of this chair and release all this pent-up energy and sweat out toxins. You don't *have* to work out. You *get* to work out."

In that embarrassing moment, Diana came to the profound realization that she had the *privilege* of exercising, and that exercise was something she *got* to do, not something she should feel *obligated* to do.

I suggest to my clients that they treat exercise the same way they treat brushing their teeth--something you just get up and do every day, to protect your health, and because you always feel better as a result. Exercise affects everything: our body image, our self-esteem, and our sense of pride in taking care of ourselves.

Exercise also triggers endorphins and serotonin manufactured by the body's own internal chemistry set. This is the perfect way to experience a healthful, powerful "high."

By the way, another benefit of exercise is that it burns calories. But don't exercise just for that reason, or even primarily for that reason. Do it because it's good for every aspect of your life! It's simply something that needs to become a natural part of your healthy life, because the way you *approach* things has a direct correlation to your results. Let's take a moment and review what we've discussed. We've seen that the multi-billion dollar diet industry has a lot invested in keeping you on the endless diet treadmill. We've seen that your bathroom scale doesn't tell you anything valid about your eating. And we've seen that by paying attention to what satiates you-- what makes you feel full and contented--you can eat whatever you want (no more forbidden foods) and you can arrive easily and without dieting at your body's natural healthy weight. Best of all, you can stay at that weight without yo-yoing, without "starting a new diet," and without guilt.

It all sounds simple...maybe even <u>too</u> simple. Since that's the case, let's explore the underlying ideas and beliefs that many people have about weight loss and their lives...ideas and beliefs that may actually be keeping you from your ideal weight...and your ideal life.

Part Two

Why Un-Dieting Works:

Removing the Psychological Barriers to Weight Loss

Chapter Five -- Getting Complete With Incompletions

Chances are that this is not the first book that you have ever read about food and dieting. It's very rare for a client to come to me without an extensive background in diet literature as well as experiences with all kinds of diets. Wherever you turn today, you find another diet--in a bookstore, in virtually every women's magazine, on TV, and even listening to the radio in your car. We are literally surrounded by diets. And yet we suffer because diets simply don't work.

Everyone who has ever dieted, whether once, twenty times, or for a lifetime, knows, deep down in his or her soul, that *diets don't work*. The multi-billion dollar diet industry depends on our continuing to believe, persistently and unrelentingly, that some new diet WILL WORK. That's how they keep us on the treadmill of buying every new fad diet that comes along. That's how they keep their multi-billion dollar industry growing each and every year. It also explains why we find ourselves stopping by the diet counters of stores in our constant search for the new breakthrough diet or pill that will finally put us out of our dieting misery. America, in short, has become a nation of hungry dieters.

We are all obsessed with getting thinner. We're so hungry, from the dieting/binge cycle that we described in earlier chapters, that when we do eat, our portions are so large that we consume more and more calories...which is the only real way to gain weight. The problem is that even if we do understand that dieting doesn't work, based on our own experiences or that of our friends, relatives, neighbors, or even talk show hosts, we still do it! We still keep thinking that the magic bullet diet is right around the corner. The reason diets fail us is because weight gain and loss usually has little or nothing to do with food. We don't know how to get down to our natural body weight, and stay there, and we haven't learned to accept our own natural body weight. It's because we don't know how to deal with the emotions and feelings that cause us to eat and to overeat.

Feelings that keep us on the weight loss/weight gain treadmill are what I call *incompletions*.

Feelings that keep us on the weight loss/weight gain treadmill are what I call *incompletions*.

The psychological principle of "repetition compulsion" basically means that we have a tendency to repeat anything in our life that we haven't come to terms with, that we haven't mastered, that remains incomplete. Frequently, when we overeat, we bust a diet that had been going well for a period of weeks, or even a month or two. We have been driven to the refrigerator or the convenience store to buy so-called forbidden foods and gorge ourselves on them. What drove us to this self-destructive, painful act?

Many times, it's because we were triggered by these painful, unresolved feelings and situations in our lives called incompletions. We need to recognize the enormous power of incompletions to keep us from enjoying life fully, from reaching and maintaining our natural ideal body weight, and even from enjoying our love relationships and work situations as fully as possible. In this chapter, we are going to learn all about incompletions, and how they keep us from where we want to go. Most important, we will learn how to resolve them so they lose their power over us and so that we can reach and maintain that natural body weight.

First, a story.

Elaine, forty-seven, has been the vice president of a bank for the past seventeen years, making a six figure income. One day, all of a sudden, she quit her job. She came into my office shortly after quitting, and expressed her sense of terror about the future. How would she pay her bills? What would she do next? People don't simply up and quit great jobs for no reason, and she was terrified as to how the working world--not to mention her husband, friends, and family--would react to her sudden and seemingly inexplicable career move.

Everyone was telling her she was crazy for quitting, and her eating, not surprisingly, was out of control. In a period of five months after leaving that job, she gained thirty-five pounds.

I asked Elaine why she quit her job. We talked for some time--actually, it took four sessions before the truth came out. She confided to me that six years earlier, on a business trip, her boss had raped her. As she told me the story I felt the hair on the back of my neck standing up. I was getting a signal from somewhere--probably intuition--that this was not the first time that she had been sexually assaulted. I asked her, "And this isn't the first time you were raped, is it?"

Elaine started to cry. Through her tears, she said that someone had molested her when she was six years old. It had only happened one time, but she had never forgotten it. When I asked her who had done it, she appeared perplexed for quite a while. She sat in silence for a few long minutes. Then her eyes widened and she looked up at me and said, quietly and calmly, "It was my father!"

Elaine had never before faced the fact, or told anyone, that her father had done this to her. She told me that he never did it again. They never even spoke about it. She remained very close to him, and thirteen years later, he committed suicide. He left her a note, which said, in part, "You, above everyone else, can understand why I had to do this."

Elaine's brutal experience, as a child, and then on that business trip, had enormous ramifications for every aspect of her life, including her personal life and relationships, and her relationship with food. Let's take a look at some of the ramifications of this traumatic incompletion in Elaine's life:

1) She never told her husband about either incident, which means there are large secrets in their relationship. Secrets like this can greatly inhibit full intimacy.

2) In the workplace, for six years on a daily basis, she faced a man who had violated her, betrayed her, and taken away any

sense of safety. In addition, she no longer believed that her continuing tenure at the bank was due to the high quality of her job performance. Rather, she came to believe that her boss was simply too scared to fire her, fearing a lawsuit. Doubts and apprehensions replaced her feelings of fulfillment about a job that she had always done extremely well.

3) She could not understand why she was depressed and angry all the time.

4) She ate all the time, and yet was always hungry. She gained weight and couldn't fit into her clothes.

5) She was preoccupied. (Who wouldn't be?)

6) She neglected her friendships, feeling very isolated. Certainly, since she couldn't tell her husband, she couldn't tell anyone else. So her secrets got bigger and bigger because there was no one with whom to share it or resolve it.

7) She lost all respect for herself, and her self-esteem fell to an all-time low.

8) She felt no direction for the future.

9) She obsessively thought about revenge.

In short, it is not a coincidence that the same thing that happened to Elaine when she was a small child happened to her again in the workplace. Anything that we don't come to terms with is likely to reappear in our lives down the road. Both of these events--the assault by Elaine's father and the rape by her boss--constitute extremely painful and traumatic incompletions. The good news is that it is possible to resolve these incompletions, and Elaine did. Before we see the rest of her story, let's take a deeper look at exactly what incompletions are all about.

As I said earlier, "repetition compulsion" means that we have a tendency to repeat whatever in our life we have not mastered--whatever remains incomplete. This explains a lot of otherwise seemingly inexplicable behavior, such as women who are battered as children who end up in a series of relationships in adulthood where they are physically or emotionally abused, like Elaine. These women keep finding themselves in the same or similar circumstances, even though they hate everything about it. They may be drawn to situations in which they are victimized because such situations have an aspect of familiarity. If a young child is repeatedly victimized, that child may repeat that victimization over and over as an adult, for two basic reasons: 1) This is what the child, grown to adulthood, is "comfortable" with--this is what he or she knows best; and/or 2) It is an incompletion (something not mastered, not clean, not handled in some way).

What are incompletions? They may be things you haven't communicated that you know you need to communicate. They may be things that you've said or done that hurt or otherwise negatively affected other people. They may be things that others have done to hurt you. Incompletions also include things you feel ashamed of, things for which you don't forgive yourself, things you've done that compromised your values and integrity, things that somehow need cleaning up.

Whatever is incomplete stays on your mind. It saps your energy. You may not be thinking about it all the time, but it's always there. That incompletion occupies your subconscious mind. **Whatever is in our subconscious mind directs the way we think and act consciously.** In short, incompletions keep you from being fully present to your own life.

....

Whatever is in our subconscious mind directs the way we think and act consciously.

....

How do most people handle incompletions? Well, it probably won't surprise you to learn that one of the most successful ways to avoid looking at an incompletion is to stuff it down with food. After the binging party is over, you may tend to focus on your guilt over what you ate, your shame about it, your lack of willpower, or maybe even how pathetic you are. By remaining on this cycle of unconscious focus on an incompletion, binge eating, and then the aftermath of guilt, shame, and self-hatred, the incompletion actually continues to exist unabated. We call this avoidance.

Avoidance is more fattening than German chocolate cake. Avoidance packs more calories than the richest, creamiest dessert you can imagine, because avoidance cannot be dieted away. The only way to get off that cycle of incompletion, binge eating, remorse, and further avoidance, is by facing squarely whatever incompletion leads us back to the cycle in the first place.

··

Avoidance is more fattening than German chocolate cake. Avoidance packs more calories than the richest, creamiest dessert you can imagine, because avoidance cannot be dieted away.

··

In my experience as a therapist, I have found it very common for women and men to have sexual abuse at the root of their troubles with food. Sexual abuse is certainly one of the most powerful, frightening and compelling forms of incompletion that an individual can face. But incompletions are not always about sexual abuse, and millions of individuals who, fortunately, never experienced sexual abuse, still suffer from other kinds of painful incompletions in their life. Here are some examples:

A) You had an argument with the person who was once your best friend, and the two of you haven't spoken for years.

B) You said something to someone that wasn't really the truth. You wonder if you'll get caught.

C) You gossiped about a friend.

D) You were attacked by someone and never turned them into the police.

E) You and your sibling or a friend engaged in sexual experimentation as kids.

F) You caused an accident on a highway where someone was hurt, but you left the scene and you were never arrested or even implicated.

It's never easy to look back in our lives and identify the incompletions that we carry with us. It's never easy to go to the people we hurt and say we are sorry, or to otherwise right an old wrong. Often, the experiences underlying these incompletions are the most painful memories we have, which is why we work so hard to suppress them in the first place. After twenty years of clinical experience, however, I can assure you that as hard as it may be to resolve an incompletion, it is much harder to live *without* doing so. It's virtually impossible to have a healthy relationship with people, food, work, money, alcohol, sex, or any other substance or subject in our lives if major incompletions are hanging over our heads. This is why I recommend as strongly as I possibly can that you take time to look at the incompletions in your life, face them head on, and do whatever repair work is necessary so that they no longer dog your every step, trouble your unconscious, and dictate the way you relate to people and food.

....

As hard as it may be to resolve an incompletion, it is much harder to live *without* doing so.

....

Here are some examples of some possible completions for the six incompletions I just enumerated:

A) You call your ex-best friend, and tell her how you are responsible for your part in whatever the problem was. You ask if the two of you can sit down together to talk and see if you can get that relationship back on track. Incidentally, there is a difference between accepting responsibility for one's actions, which is healthy, and sinking in blame, which keeps us trapped in the problem. We do not need to blame ourselves for events of the past. We do, however, need to take responsibility for the actions we took and their consequences. This is a subtle distinction, but it will mean the world to your mental health.

B) For the person to whom you shaded the truth or outright lied: call that person and tell the truth now. Explain that you didn't tell the complete truth back then. Don't beat yourself up over it, and don't even worry about whether the person accepts your apology for having lied. What matters is that you are cleaning up your side of the street. If the other person is magnanimous and forgives you, so much the better. But keep in mind that you do not need someone else's forgiveness to gain that sense of completion. All you need to do is to go back and make amends for the actions that you took back then that bother you today.

C) If you gossiped, you can clean up that situation by apologizing to two people--the person to whom you gossiped, and the person about whom you gossiped. Whenever we gossip, we actually hurt two people. We hurt the person we are subjecting to our gossip, because we are negatively affecting the way that person views the third party about whom we are speaking. We may be damaging an otherwise wonderful relationship, simply because we are feeling insecure or envious, spiteful or malicious. So we go to the person to whom we gossiped and we apologize, not with a sense of moral superiority--"Now I'm above gossiping, I hope you are, too"--but instead with a simple sense of humility. "I did something wrong, I feel bad about it, and I want to tell you that I am sorry." In so doing, we must also promise we will not continue that behavior in the future.

We also may want to apologize to the person about whom we gossiped, because we have hurt that person's reputation in the community, in the family, in the workplace, or in whatever situation we know that person. This is a delicate matter, however, so we want to be very careful that we are not going to cause further insult or injury by bringing the matter up to the person who might not have known that he or she was the subject of our forked tongue. So exercise caution in this area. We can never get a sense of completion or mental health at the expense of another person, especially a person we have already harmed.

D) If you were attacked by someone, discuss with a professional whether it is now appropriate at this time to make a police report. There is a tendency for people who see themselves as victims to believe that they have no rights. This is not the case. No matter what you have been through, no matter how painful, you have the same rights to enjoy your life as anyone else on the planet. This is your time to explore whether your rights were violated, and if so, whether it is appropriate now to take further action. We do not want to act out of a sense of vindictiveness though. There is an unhealthy sense of power and rage that comes from acting on a desire or urge to punish. Instead of acting on that impulse immediately, I suggest that you discuss the whole event with a trained professional, and together work out a plan to best handle the violation of your rights.

E) If you and a sibling or friend engaged in childhood sexual experimentation, you're not alone. Millions of children do so, either maliciously or simply out of curiosity. It's not the end of the world. It may be appropriate nonetheless for you to have a conversation with that person, in order to discuss the matter. This may sound strange, but in most cases like this I do not advocate blame or pointing the finger. I strongly believe in speaking the truth to the important people in our lives, whoever they are. It is possible to speak the truth even to people who have hurt us a long time ago, and come away from the exchange healed and whole. Chances are we will even be doing the other person a great service, because the act or acts that person committed are probably a painful incompletion in his or her life as well.

There is a difference between angry confrontations and reasoned conversations. You will find that if you approach the person in a reasonable way, and without blame, you can accomplish powerful healing. You may be able to effect a resolution to this nightmare that has been hanging over your life and deeply affecting the way you relate to people, food, and everything else. Again, though, if you were the victim of molestation or sexual assault, I urge you to discuss this with a trained professional before you seek to have a conversation about the matter with the person who perpetrated the act.

F) If you caused an accident or otherwise "got away" with something that you are not proud of, the question you have to ask yourself is whether you really got away with it. Frequently, my clients beat themselves up and punish themselves far more painfully than the law ever could, even if there had been a policeman standing right over the situation. Our inner prosecutor, inner policeman, and inner jailor combine to mete out punishments usually far more painful than anything that could be assessed in a court of law.

The time for self-punishment is over. Instead of destructively beating ourselves up for what has happened and what cannot be undone, what can we do in order to handle the situation in a constructive manner? Perhaps we can do some volunteer work with children, or battered women, or the homeless, or some other group of individuals who need our help. Perhaps there is some sort of community service that we can perform. It is time to stop beating yourself up for the past. The only way to have a happy present is to give up all hope of a happier past. See what kind of restitution you can make, either to the individual you harmed, or to society as a whole, and then quit beating yourself up.

....

The only way to have a happy present is to give up all hope of a happier past.

....

Most people are terrified of completions and avoid them. We have a tendency to justify in our minds why we don't need to get complete with a particular situation. The more painful that situation was, the greater our ability to justify avoiding it. We might tell ourselves that the whole thing will turn into a "confrontation" and we have a million reasons for avoiding confrontation. In ninety percent of the cases, however, incompletions never turn into upsetting confrontations. Most people are so touched that we have come to them, hat in hand, to resolve a situation, that they actually treat us with newfound respect and admiration.

Sometimes when we want to avoid a completion, we'll say things to ourselves like "I'll feel like an idiot!" Or, "She'll think I'm an idiot!" Or, "I'll make a fool of myself!" "I'll just provoke her anger!" "I'm probably just making a big deal about nothing!" "I'll just cause myself bigger problems!" Most of these justifications exist simply because we are terrified of completions. We are also afraid to admit to having made mistakes. We are afraid to say, "I don't understand. We fear looking stupid, silly, or different. So with all these fears going on, we ardently avoid completion, and we just pretend everything is okay.

But everything is not okay. Incompletions are actually breaches of our own integrity. We have done something that we know deep down was not okay to do. So we justify it to ourselves rather than handling it, fixing it, or just taking responsibility for it. Avoidance of an incompletion just keeps us suffering. We suffer because our body and mind know that the situation is not complete. Our body/mind keeps telling us that we have left this situation incomplete, and those messages may take the form of aches and pains in our body and our psyche. And we will act out those situations again and again, in different forms and with different people. That's why the psychological term for this is "repetition compulsion."

The really big problem with incompletions is that once a pattern of avoidance is learned we then continue to pile on more and more incompletions. We never realize how much we are hurting ourselves until we either have a heart attack or some other serious wake-up signal that tells us we haven't been handling our life very well! We honestly believed that everything was okay, but we eat way too much and obsess about our body, our blood pressure is high, we get stress headaches, we don't get along with people at work, we experience frequent illness, depression, and lack of energy. That's the price we pay for avoidance. Denial and avoidance, when practiced often, lead to other forms of lying to ourselves. Many people come into therapy in mid-life because they feel that "all of a sudden, life became unmanageable." They never realized that they created that unmanageableness slowly and methodically every time they denied that something was going on.

Speaking of incompletions, remember Elaine, the woman who was raped by her boss? Here's how she started getting complete. First, I asked her to write a letter to her deceased father, telling him how much he hurt her, first when he molested her, and then when he committed suicide. She read the letter to me with deep emotion, and in the end, was able to say she forgave him. Next was the issue of the rape by her ex-boss. She finally told her husband, who surprised her with tremendous understanding and support. Since the Statute of Limitations had passed on this crime she was unable to file a lawsuit. But she found a sympathetic attorney who was able to file a claim against him under Workers' Compensation, whereupon Elaine was at least able to take the issue public. She was then able to declare the incident over, so that she could begin living again.

I would like to share with you an example from my own life. Shortly after my husband and I were married, his mother developed Alzheimer's disease. She slowly fell into dementia, but the family was in denial, and would correct everything she said, as if she understood and could fix it. After listening to this for quite a while, I finally told my father-in-law one evening that his wife doesn't understand him anymore. Instead of correcting her, he should just help her. And I told him that he should stop expecting her to be who she used to be. This was one of those moments where it got really, really quiet in the room. After about a minute, my father-in-law finally spoke. Instead of responding to the comment I made, which obviously took me a great deal of courage to express, he remarked about how beautiful the weather was! And then my husband joined in and responded, "Yeah, it's beautiful out."

I felt for a few moments as if I had gone crazy. All of a sudden I felt alone, stupid, and totally unsupported. I felt like the boy who shouted "The Emperor has no clothes!" I couldn't handle their decision to completely ignore the fact that I had made a comment about this very painful and troubling situation. I said, out loud, "Did anyone hear me? Did anyone here hear me?" Then I told them I was willing to drop the subject, or to hear their feelings, but I just wanted to know that they heard me.

My husband looked as though he had been awakened from a decades-long slumber. He realized that what went on in his family might have been the way they handled things, but that he had a responsibility to me as his wife not to subject me to that same kind of denial and, quite frankly, bizarre behavior. My husband responded directly to what I said and told me that yes, he and his father had heard me. I felt so relieved. I thought I was losing my mind. The discussion about my mother-in-law continued for some time and got complete. We went on to have a wonderful evening.

Later that night, when we were alone, I asked my husband if his family had a tendency to not talk about what's happening and instead go into denial. He said, "Always! Why do you think I have such a strained relationship with the members of my family?...we can't talk to each other!" My husband was actually grateful that I had come along and interrupted a pattern that had enveloped his entire family life from his earliest childhood.

Believe me, ten or fifteen years earlier, I would never have had the courage to confront that rather bizarre situation the way I did. I would have done what most people would have done--I would have thought to myself, are these people crazy, or am I? And I probably would have decided that I was the crazy one. I would have beat myself up for intruding into someone else's personal business. I would have been angry with myself for overstepping my boundaries. In other words, I would have found a way to justify my father-in-law's rather weird reaction-- his complete pretending that I had not even commented on his wife's Alzheimer's. I would have made myself wrong for what I had done. I would have made him the normal, healthy one, and I would have made myself the bad guy.

The fact is that *there are no bad guys*, even in situations like this. Everyone is always doing the best they can, based on whatever information and experience they already possess. At that point in time, the best my father-in-law could do was pretend that I had not even raised the issue. The whole thing was far too painful for him to bear. Today, I am very grateful that I have progressed to the point where I was able to confront that situation immediately, while it was still going on. I did not need to make myself bad or wrong. I did not need to make anyone else bad or wrong either. That's very important. I have a wonderful relationship with my father-in-law. Once again, I cannot win my mental health at the cost of other people's peace of mind. Instead, I was able to find a middle path between playing along with the denial that anything was wrong and angrily confronting the people I loved. I was able to simply state my need, which was to ask whether or not anyone had heard me. As a result, I did not create a brand new incompletion which I would eat over and beat myself up over in days, months, and even years to come.

Not creating new incompletions is in itself incredibly freeing! It means that I'm not creating new wreckage in my life. It means that I have the emotional energy to live my life in the present moment to the fullest--while cleaning up whatever incompletions from the past still need my attention.

....

Not creating new incompletions is in itself incredibly freeing! It means that I'm not creating new wreckage in my life.

....

The point is that when something is "going on with us," when something is disturbing or weird or strange, that's a signal. If we pay attention to those signals, they will usually lead us in the right direction. When we disregard signals, it's called denial. When we start practicing denial, denial becomes our pattern, our habit, the place where we go all the time in order to feel safe.

Unfortunately, when we practice denial, we soon lose ourselves in the process. When we live in denial, we become an actor, and eventually we feel unsure of what's real and what's not real. The result of living in denial is that we agonize with ourselves, in our own mind, all the time. This is called prison! And many people who end up in this prison...eat, in order to keep shoving down feelings.

Incidentally, I felt a renewed respect for my husband after experiencing his family's pattern of denial. That's because I found it to be so crazy-making, even after just a few minutes. I was suddenly awestruck by my husband's courage in choosing me as his spouse, because I'm a person who needs to discuss and confront everything!

Incompletions drain our energy! This is the key fact for us. The reason that incompletions drain our energy is that until something is complete it remains on our mind. Anything on our mind takes energy. When we build up numerous incompletions, we feel overwhelmed, exhausted, and drained. This explains why so many people go through life feeling so swamped and so tired. I'd like you know that most tiredness is not really tiredness--it's more of a feeling of overwhelm. We feel as though life is handing us too much stuff, when really it's us who are responsible. We're not handling, or completing, things in our own life. We are wasting enormous amounts of energy fretting and revisiting and giving up ground to those incompletions. Incompletions truly drain our energy.

....

Incompletions truly drain our energy.

....

Incompletions not only affect our relationship with ourselves--they deeply affect our relationships with other people. When we feel incomplete, we tend to project that incompletion onto others around us simply because we are incomplete.

My client Bonnie is a top television writer. In a session she told me how mad she was at her sister, because her sister would not allow Bonnie's boyfriend in her house. Bonnie was furious that her sister was so judgmental. In the very next sentence,

Bonnie told me how repulsed she was by her sister's husband because "He's fat." Bonnie herself is considerably overweight, yet judges other people with weight problems. For Bonnie, being judgmental is an incompletion. Until and unless she transforms this judgmentalness in herself, she will always feel judged by other people. She will also always notice and dislike this quality in other people. By facing, head on, her incompletion around the issue of judgmentalness, she was able to release that judgmentalness, and feel better about herself and about her relationships with other people. Not so incidentally, she lost thirty five pounds.

The wonderful news about incompletions is that when we actually face them and complete them, the act of completing them energizes us. I'm sure you've had a taste of this, on days when you made a giant list of things to do, and you started completing them one by one. You could feel the energy that came when you started checking things off your list. It inspired you to do more because you wanted more of those good feelings that come with completion...and then you wanted to finish everything on your list.

Well, we're talking about handling situations that are a lot more draining of energy than the normal sorts of things that make it onto our daily to-do lists. We're talking about healing old relationships, forgiving ourselves and others, and righting old wrongs. Imagine how wonderful you will feel, psychologically and emotionally, after years of not handling these incompletions, after years of practicing more and more denial--imagine how good you will feel when you complete these things and send them packing. You will feel so much energy that you will be amazed!

After feeling so great about taking care of these incompletions, you'd think we would want to avoid new incompletions. But here's where that twelve-step definition of insanity comes in: "Insanity is doing the same thing over and over again and expecting different results." Even though we now know how to handle things, when new, uncomfortable situations arise, whether at work or at home, our first inclination--our natural drift--is to go *right* for the denial. It takes a lot of practice to change something that's been solidified for so many years. Not only that, there's a strong consensus in the world in favor of living in denial. Don't rock the boat, don't make waves, don't go there. So the idea here is to list your incompletions. Don't worry--you don't have to commit to handle them all now. You simply need to look them in the eye and write them down, every one of them. You will feel indescribably good when you take care of this! We're removing the weight of your incompletions from your shoulders...so that the weight from your body can melt away!

Exercise

List all the incompletions in your life, from your earliest possible memory.

(Examples: "I stole Johnny's balloon in the third grade." "I never apologized to my girlfriend for getting drunk at her wedding,"etc.)

_____

_____

_____

_____

_____

_____

_____

_____

_____

_____

I promise to handle every one of these completions within a period of time not to exceed six months.

_____   _____
Signature   Date

(Why sign your name? Because it works!!!)

Chapter Six -- Forgiveness is a Choice

It may not seem likely or even possible, but there is a powerful connection between forgiveness and eating. Let's take a look at just what that connection is, and how understanding it can change your whole life, not just your relationship with food.

Whatever we don't forgive, we literally hold onto. Notice how many of us hold onto weight? Think there's a connection? After many years of working with people who struggle with their weight, I know for a fact that there is a very powerful connection between holding onto things we don't forgive and holding onto excess weight. Anger, which is directly connected to non-forgiveness, is the number one reason why people eat...when they're not eating out of real physical hunger.

My job as a therapist is to help people recognize the connection between the need for forgiveness and the ability to lose weight and keep that weight off. After all, what's the point of going on a diet, working hard, and losing a lot of weight, only to gain it back in far less time than it took to lose it, simply because the underlying issues that led to the initial weight gain and preoccupation with dieting were never addressed?

Let's take a closer look now at the process of forgiveness and how it relates to reaching and maintaining one's natural and proper body weight.

Myra, an extremely accomplished actress, came to me with her fiancé and said that they wanted to get some small issues handled and their communication in order before getting married. She also wanted some referrals to weight-loss centers to help her with a recent weight gain. She began by discussing her feelings of jealousy, mistrust, and fear about the viability of her relationship. She believed that any problems they had at that time were her fiancé's fault. She pointed out to me his attention to other people, his enjoyment of "bimbo-type women" (her phrase) on television, and his obvious lack of respect for women in general.

This is a perfect example of "projection." Myra's upset about the lack of respect for women she felt her fiancé evidenced was actually Myra's problem with respecting women--and with respecting herself. She was unaware of this. Obviously, Myra had some issues about herself and other women, and I asked her if she could see this pattern. After a few sessions, she did see the pattern. I asked her if she wanted to get complete with it, and she agreed. It's worth mentioning that the most vital part of the completion process is that the person be ready for the process. Clearly, if you have read this far in this book, you, too are ready to complete whatever incompletions remain in your psyche. To do this, we must be willing to give up *suffering*. To give up suffering means that we need to give up our *story*. I always tell clients who are ready to do completion work that they will be telling me their *story* for the last time. That *story* is the one they've been telling for a long, long time, and the one that has been keeping them stuck in the past.

Myra and I scheduled a two hour session with instructions for homework for the night before. I sent her several newspaper articles that addressed the need to understand and come to terms with our parents and our past. Her homework was to first read the articles, and know that she would be revisiting her past and her feelings but also to know that she would be doing so for the last time. I asked her to set aside an hour and a half with no interruptions, no phone calls, no meals. She was to work with a pad of paper and a pen. At the top of each sheet of paper, I asked her to write the names of the significant people in her life with whom she was incomplete. For Myra, it was her mother, several early girlfriends, and herself. (Please note that it does not matter whether the person with whom you are incomplete is living or dead, accessible or unavailable.) Myra's next task was simply to write.

It didn't matter if she wrote a letter, jotted notes, or simply wrote "I hate you!" What matters with completion work is that we revisit our experience, with the full intensity of these childhood feelings that were not felt, or perhaps not allowed, at the time the experience took place. This means we must go back in our mind to the significant, or life-altering experiences with which we are incomplete.

84

Does this mean that Myra had to hit something or scream out loud? No, although I have often wished for an office that was soundproof enough for this. I do find it to be effective, but it is not necessary. Rather, the idea here is to have the client express her feelings, as fully as possible, in a safe environment, and with her *today brain*, rather than with the child's brain or young adult's brain that was perhaps too young and immature to understand and deal with those situations at the time they happened.

The reason for asking a client to revisit feelings from the past is that anything fully re-created begins to disappear. I do not personally believe that in most cases people need to spend lots of time revisiting the past. Usually by the time a client has come to therapy, she has already spent a sufficient amount of time suffering about the past! This last visit, the one Myra would make with me in that session, is actually what I call "the definitive visit to the past" because with it comes a shift in perspective--and completion.

When Myra was done writing the letters, her instructions were to take a bath, clear her mind with some music, go to sleep, and bring her letters to my office the next morning.

In our session the next morning, I began by telling Myra exactly what I have just told you: that whatever we are incomplete with drains us. In order to get full self-expression and full joy of life, we must be willing to find a way to get complete, get finished, make whole that situation. The alternative to completion is the need to find a way to "stuff" the feelings. And we usually do this through eating. *This feeling of needing to stuff ourselves is simply a metaphoric signal that we are not filled up or fulfilled in some way. Once we are willing to address what it is in our life that really needs fulfilling, we can do something other than eat.*

This feeling of needing to stuff ourselves is simply a metaphoric signal that we are not filled up or fulfilled in some way. Once we are willing to address what it is in our life that really needs fulfilling, we can do something other than eat.

Once I explained that point to Myra, and once she was able to agree with it, we were able to move to the next stage, which is forgiveness. It was now time for Myra to learn one of the most powerful lessons of all: that **forgiveness is a choice**. This idea is so important that it deserves its own chapter. I'm sure you'll agree with me that this concept represents a radically different, freeing, and empowering way to look at the world.

Myra came to me sick and tired of feeling uncomfortable, and she was ready to stop carrying around all that emotional pain. She was in so much pain that she was willing to do whatever it took to get rid of that discomfort and resentment. This is actually critical. Most people need to be sick and tired of holding on to their feelings of resentment or pain in order to move forward to the forgiveness process. I asked Myra what she felt sick and tired of. She replied, "I'm sick of feeling like a victim around other women, and I'm sick of this feeling of anger and jealousy."

Myra looked rather relaxed as we began our session together. Many people look drained and even listless as we begin, only to find themselves energized by the process of forgiveness and the prospect of a life without anger, resentment, and excess weight.

I asked Myra to read to me the letter she had written to her mother, and I knew that this would be the last time she would have to visit the events in this letter. She was to read with as much feeling as she could possibly put forth. (Please note, that there is no one correct way to handle this process--however she read the letter would have been fine.) Myra cried several times while reading, and I encouraged her to keep on reading right through her tears. What came out of the letter was this: Myra had several issues with her parents and her past, but the bottom line of her insecurity around other women came from a comment her mother had made when Myra started developing into a woman, around age eleven. Myra's mother told her at that time to stuff her bra "so that she would look more like a woman."

The effect of that statement to the eleven year old Myra was more traumatic than she could possibly have realized at the time. Myra spent the next thirty years trying to excel at everything...dancing, singing, acting, running a business. She took all of her own work to great heights, and appeared on Broadway. She had her own television series, and even opened her own restaurant. Nothing, however, made her feel that she was attractive enough, accomplished enough, or good enough, because, bottom line, she didn't have breasts! And the reason she was always triggered by the "bimbo-type" women she saw on television, was because they represented to her all that she was missing. This is called "projection," because she was projecting her feelings or incompletions onto others.

When Myra was complete with her letter to her mother, I read from my notes and I recreated for her exactly what she had gone through, as best I could. I told her I understood completely how the comment from her mother made her feel undesirable and inadequate, and I told her that no children should ever have to feel that they are not enough just the way they are. We discussed how it must have made her feel different, separate from other females, and how a seemingly trivial comment had affected all of her relationships with men. This was a validation process, because Myra, like all clients--like all of us--first needs to feel totally heard and understood, validated and perhaps even admired, for doing what it took to survive her traumas. This is also called "re-creating" someting, so that it can start to disappear.

We then discussed the concept of an ideal childhood, where a child is totally loved, supported, nurtured, and given all the tools for succeeding in life. I told Myra I wish I could somehow recreate for her this ideal childhood. I also told her that I could count on one hand the number of people I've met who had ideal childhoods. In other words, Myra is in good company with most other people in the world.

But then, I continued, Myra wouldn't be who she is now, without those dreadful experiences. I told her about some of my own experiences from the past, doing drugs, losing jobs, stealing...and how all of those things are a part of who I am now. In fact, those things help me to understand and better deal with other people's addictions. And I then explained that we always have a choice to do one of two things, as we start to face our issues head on: we can either use our experiences--all of them--to learn and to grow, or we can use them to justify why we can't do something. We either get to have resolution or a rationale for not having resolution. We either have results or a reason why we we aren't succeeding.

....

We either get to have *resolution* or a *rationale*. We either have results or a reason why we aren't succeeding.

....

I slowly went down a list of things that Myra's mother had said and done to her over the years. Then, I started with the least offensive item I could find on that list. I asked Myra this question: "Would you be willing to forgive her for this?"

In order to forgive, we need to have a definition of what forgiveness means and what it entails. I'd like to offer a definition that I learned many years ago, and one that I believe to be the most user-friendly and pragmatic. To forgive can simply mean to release all feelings of resentment and revenge...forever.

....

To forgive can simply mean to release all feelings of resentment and revenge...forever.

....

Does forgiveness mean that what they did was okay?
No, not necessarily.

Does it mean that we now have to be in some kind of relationship with the people we are forgiving?

Not unless you want to. There is no obligation to resume a relationship with these individuals. All we have to do is come to terms with the actions and events from the past.

Doesn't forgiveness vindicate them?

No. Absolutely not. We are not casting judgment one way or the other on what they did. We are simply releasing ourselves from the pain that our resentment triggers. (By the way, life will always take care of the people who caused us pain...but as a friend of mine says, it will not always be for your viewing pleasure!)

Forgiveness is never for the other person. It is always for you! The other person usually doesn't *know* or *care* if you're carrying around anger at him or her.

....

Forgiveness is never for the other person. It is always for you!

....

The first item on the list concerned a particular evening when Myra's mother had accused her of doing something she hadn't done. When I asked Myra if she'd be willing to forgive her mother for that, she took about ten seconds and then responded, "Yes, I could forgive her for that." I asked her how she was able to pull forth forgiveness for that item. Her reply was this: "I guess my mother just reacted to the situation, and didn't take time to gather enough facts. I guess I can forgive her because I've done that myself."

"So you forgave her?" I asked. "Because you've done something similar?"

"Yes," she replied.

We continued down the list. As Myra forgave a few more of the smaller items, I asked her each time how she was able to do so...how she was able to forgive her mother for that event or situation?

Myra would explain with answers like, "Well, she didn't know any other way to handle things," or "I guess she was just repeating what her parents did to her." Since she had now pulled forth forgiveness several times, I asked Myra where forgiveness comes from. Most people believe that forgiveness comes from their heart or their mind. I disagree. Where forgiveness comes from is simply *choice*. We seem to need to justify that choice in one way or another. But with or without justification, it's a choice! We can choose forgiveness because of any number of reasons, or we can choose it just because we don't want to suffer anymore!

With all this in mind, Myra was now able to forgive the larger items because, as she said, "I don't want to carry this around any more!" No matter what justification or reason you give for your choice to forgive, you are the beneficiary of this very wise choice. You were never punishing the other person. You were only punishing yourself, because you lost pieces of your own life! You lost time. And time is one of the most valuable commodities we have.

As soon as Myra chose to forgive, she was free. What I mean is that she was now free to choose to see herself differently. She is not less than other women. She is not deficient. And she is not unsexy. She made a new decision about herself, and declared it out loud, "My body is amazing, and it does incredible things!" She told me that until age eleven, she had always believed that. She told me now, "I have a dancer's body. I should be proud of it...and from now on I will!" Her excess weight *dropped* away without any dieting, and she feels as if her body is *"back to the way it's supposed to be."*

Myra is excited now about her upcoming marriage, and about the possibility that she and her new husband will be working together in the future. She is also excited about her new relationship with her mother, because she feels more connected and less reactive to her.

Here's another example of projection and how it disrupts family relationships. Edna is a sixty-six year old grandmother. Her daughter Lucy married an African-American man. Edna came to me at the request of her daughter Lucy after Edna had repeatedly refused to have anything to do with either Lucy's husband or with Lucy's two children. Edna told me that she was angry at her child Lucy for marrying a black man, because of the anger that would be directed at the children of that union. Edna did not realize that she was acting cruelly toward her own grandchildren by refusing to see them, bringing about the very situation she claimed to be angry at her daughter for causing.

Edna could not see her own prejudice reflected in her anger. Whatever we are, we believe others are. Whatever we haven't forgiven, both of ourselves and others, we are stuck with! Whatever we despise about others is really some aspect of ourselves we are unwilling to examine. It is a cruel twist from God to give us exactly what we give the world. Whatever we see in other people that we don't like is *almost always* something we are refusing to look at in ourselves.

....

Whatever we see in other people that we don't like is *almost always* something we are refusing to look at in ourselves.

....

If you wish to move your life forward, find a way to get complete with everyone and everything from your past.

Let's do this exercise together.

1) With whom and with what are you incomplete in your life? (This is the perfect moment to review the list you made when you did the exercise in Chapter Three.)

2) For each item, would you be willing to get complete by forgiving that person or yourself, so that you can move forward with your life?

3) If you don't forgive that person, what is your payoff? What reward, benefit, or perk do you get? If you don't forgive, what's in it for you? (By the way, the number one payoff for people is that they get to be right about that situation. Is being right that valuable to you?)

4) Take time now to write a letter or speak words of forgiveness out loud to each of the people on your list. Tell them that you don't necessarily approve of what they did, if you like,

but tell them that you forgive them and that you are releasing all of your negativity and anger toward them, now and forever.

If you have forgiven yourself and others, using this exercise,

CONGRATULATIONS! You are now free! (At least on those items!) Let's talk for a moment about the people whom you might not have been ready to put down on this list. Since you're in the swing of it here, this is a really good time to move on to forgive them as well. **If you're not there yet, just keep in mind that *not* forgiving is *also* a choice.** It is important to acknowledge that we are choosing something even if we're choosing *not* to forgive, so that we can no longer look at ourselves as victims. If you haven't forgiven, you might want to perhaps pretend you've forgiven, just for a moment, to see how it feels. And know that you can always choose forgiveness later. There are no time limits on anything to do with the human soul.

Chapter Seven -- The High Cost of Being Right

People who want to be in a great relationship often talk about their quest for Mr. Right or Ms. Right. There's nothing wrong with wanting to find the right person. That's what the quest for love is all about. The trouble comes when we find the right person, and then we have to *be* right--about everything--all the time!

Nothing is more annoying than people who have to be right. There are cancers of the body, and there are also cancers of the mind. In my opinion, the compulsion to be right is one of the most self-destructive cancers of the mind that could possibly exist. Let's examine this soul-deadening compulsion to be right.

....

The compulsion to be right is one of the most self-destructive cancers of the mind that could possibly exist.

....

Everybody has a story. By story, I mean those beliefs that you have been hanging on to and that you repeat over and over in your head until you actually make them come true. And they *always* come true! That's why these beliefs are often called self-fulfilling prophecies.

One of the most useful things you can do for yourself is identify those areas of your life in which you feel a compulsion to be right. I want you to see the price that you are paying for hanging on, perhaps unconsciously, to the story that you have told yourself over and over again. The best way I can illustrate this concept is to give you an example from my own life.

I write this story with the full permission of my wonderful and adorable mother, whom I love and respect more than anything. One of our favorite private family jokes (soon to be not so private!) was that my mother always became constipated when she travelled. Growing up, I often heard colorful stories about her needing enemas in places like Japan and China. When she talked about it, either to herself or others, she never realized that her mind was *locking in* a concept called "You always get constipated when you travel." Her body, of course, would always agree with that concept. I always enjoyed these stories until a few years ago--when I began to live the story for myself.

My husband and I were vacationing in Yosemite National Park. We were sitting in a beautiful wide-open area, watching deer, when my husband whispered to me, "I'd better find an outhouse." I knew he had just gone to the bathroom an hour earlier, and I'd been somewhat constipated since the night before. I said to him, "Boy, you're so lucky...I'd give anything to go just once!" And a second later, I found myself saying, out loud, "Oh, my God, I've become my mother!" What frightened me at that moment was the fact that somehow somewhere along the way I had created the same malady as my mother without even knowing it. I now had her symptoms, not mine. I was saying her words, not mine. Even when you love your mother dearly, as I do, it doesn't necessarily mean that you wish to have all her traits. And this was one I definitely didn't want.

Fortunately, I had already learned the power of changing my thoughts and beliefs. So I chose to make something happen in my life at that moment. My exact words to my somewhat surprised husband were, "I want to make a commitment to you. From now on, my body runs like a well-oiled machine. I'm a perfect-running machine." In a few moments, there were two of us running to find the outhouse.

As crazy as this may seem, it was simply a matter of understanding that the mind takes its programming literally. If you program yourself, either consciously or subconsciously, which is done every time we *fear* something, then that is what you will end up with. In other words, what we *fear*, we end up creating, because fear *is* practicing and rehearsing for failure. So, if you feel that you might get constipated when you travel because your mother did, then your mind will seek to make you right. Your mind will *always* find a way to make you right.

••

What we *fear* we end up creating, because fear *is* practicing and rehearsing for failure.

••

Programming comes *most often* in the form of fears, as in, "I'm afraid of some day getting Alzheimer's, or cancer, or diabetes, or some other terrible disease." Fears are the number one way to program ourselves, because they are habitual and pervasive, and again, anything we practice enough we will become good at creating. Now I understood that I was walking around with this concept--that I had a compulsion to be right about the way my body became constipated when I traveled. My awareness of that concept allowed me to consciously stop the programming, by replacing it with new programming. I was able to end instantaneously this family multi-generational constipation thing that probably went back several earlier generations. I've never since experienced any problems with my body's proper functioning when I travel, or at home. In other words, I had the courage to face the story that I had told myself and to recognize that my need to be right was actually hurting *me*.

"What's your story?" is a question that asks you to consider what you have bought into. What stories do you tell yourself about your life? What do you believe about yourself that keeps coming true for you? Because anything you tell yourself over and over again, whether it has to do with constipation, in my case, or your ability to lose excess weight, to succeed at work or in love, will come true if you tell yourself that thing over and over again. In other words, if you have a compulsion to be right about anything in your life, your mind will find a way to make you correct. And that's the source of so much suffering--the unexamined need to be right overpowers and overshadows our ability to be happy, to lose weight, or to succeed.

....

The unexamined need to be right overpowers and overshadows our ability to be happy, to lose weight, or to succeed.

....

In my years of counseling people, I have found that the single greatest need that men and women have is to be right! How important is that compulsion to be right? I have seen people lose business relationships in order to be right. I have seen people lose close family relationships in order to be right. I have even seen a woman make a decision to die to be right. This was a woman who refused to forgive her family for something they did to her, despite the fact that cancer was literally eating away at her body, and despite the fact that being right was alienating her from the only people she really loved! Malachy McCourt said "Resentment [staying angry at someone else] is like taking poison and waiting for the other person to die".

....

"Resentment [staying angry at someone else] is like taking poison and waiting for the other person to die"

....

Generally, the more insecure we are, the stronger our need to be right. Needing to be right goes hand in hand with needing to feel in control. Needing to be right is necessary, even essential, for anyone who considers himself or herself a victim. There are several things that could be behind this need to be right. First, the notion that there is a definite right and wrong to every issue. We all know people who see the world in very black-and-white terms. Once they make up their mind, there's no getting through to them. It can be very frustrating talking to people like that!

Second, there could be an overall feeling of not being valued, noticed, or taken seriously, and so being right may feel like the only thing we have with which to validate our sense of being okay. Third, the need to be right could be the direct result of dominating or righteous parents or siblings who themselves always needed to be right. Fourth, it could be the fact that sometimes it just becomes a habit for a person to blame others and need to be right. And there are many other possible reasons.

Whatever the reasons, as the years pass, the need to be right usually becomes more ingrained, more intense, and more urgent. And as that need increases, so does one's preoccupation with it, until being right becomes a full-time job. Those people have to make sure that no matter what, they are never wrong. Can you see how this trait can take over and dominate every interaction, every move, every friendship, every moment?

As the years pass, the need to be right usually becomes more ingrained, more intense, and more urgent.

Think about it. It takes tremendous effort to be right! Have you ever awakened with the thought, "I can't remember if we resolved that disagreement or I'm still angry."? When you remember you're angry, it actually takes work to keep that going!

Here are some examples of common beliefs that many of us have to keep on being right about, even at the cost of our serenity, our relationships, our body image, and even our lives:

* "I can't lose weight...I have no willpower."
* My parents did it to me!"
* My ex did it to me."
* I eat because of what's been done to me."
* I have such bad luck--everything bad happens to me!"
* Everyone in my family is fat--it's a genetic thing."
* "I'll never be successful--that's what my dad always said."
* "I just have a slow metabolism"
* Everyone else can lose weight, but not me! No matter what I try, nothing ever really works."

Pretty sad, huh? Let me ask you a question. Does the shoe fit? Have you ever heard yourself making any of these excuses to yourself or to other people about why your life is not exactly where you want it to be? It's okay. It's practically universal. But the good news is that we can change.

Let me tell you another story about myself. When I was four years old, my parents moved us to a small island in the Miami Beach area. As soon as the movers took my bicycle off the moving van, I rode up the block, where I saw two little girls my age. I excitedly rode over to them. But as I approached, I heard them laughing. I don't know why I felt this way, and I certainly had no evidence for this conclusion, but I was certain that they were laughing at me. I turned my bike around, rode off, and cried. I made two decisions that day that would haunt me for the next forty years--number one, I don't fit in, and number two, I'm fat, too fat for anyone to love.

I can't explain how I made these two decisions. I just did. Possibly the only difference I saw between those girls and me is that I was larger. For whatever reason, from that moment on, I became--in my mind, which is what matters--the fat girl who didn't fit in. Whenever I looked into my full-length mirror, all I could see was that I hated my lips, I hated my nose, I hated my thighs, I hated my butt, etc., and the end of each conversation that I had with myself was, "...and I'm fat." Even when I was ninety nine pounds, deeply anorexic, and in a life-threatening condition, I still felt fat.

For all those years, I kept on being right, in my own mind, about "not fitting in" and "not being enough." When you believe something long enough and hard enough, you literally make it happen...over and over again. Here's how I did it. Deep down, I felt that nobody really wanted to be my friend, so I would try even harder to be liked. To try harder meant that I had to make up stories about myself and my family so that I could brag.

My father was in the caulking business, which means that he manufactured putty. I decided to add a little something extra to make it sound more important--I told people my father invented Silly Putty! I actually told people that! What do people do when they find out that someone has just lied to them? They are repelled! I literally chased people away...all to be right. "See?" I was thus able to say to myself. "Nobody likes me. I don't fit in." I had taken the exact actions necessary in order to support the belief that I had ingrained in myself the day I rode my bicycle up to those two little girls.

Did I know I was doing this? Of course not. Do we realize we're needing to be right while we're doing it? Heck, no. To the contrary, we always believe that negative results are *happening* to us. We believe things are happening to us, and we don't realize that we're actually *creating* them by rehearsing them over and over in our minds. I was rehearsing for people not liking me, without even knowing it. People work so hard to keep on being right, even though the behavior is clearly destructive and dysfunctional, simply because it is unexamined.

In order to solve this problem, we need first to bring this subconscious material up to the level of consciousness, and then we need to harness that energy into a way that makes being right work for you! In other words, we need to do some reverse engineering on our own minds. Here's a three-step process to handle the problem of being right:

1) First we look for the result we're unhappy with. We look to find an aspect of our lives that gives us little or no pleasure.

2) Our next step is to ascertain what faulty or dysfunctional conversation we've been having with ourselves...in order to make ourselves right. Sometimes this takes a while.

3) Once you finally admit that you're having this conversation, the next step is then to turn that conversation around one husndred eighty degrees. Let me show you how.

The "truth" I told myself, that I didn't fit in anywhere, showed up repeatedly in my adult life in the workplace. I found myself moving from job to job to job, and always because there was one person in each company who was making my life miserable, usually a person in authority. After I had left my umpteenth job, I had a conversation with my mother that changed everything for me. She sat me down in her back yard, looked me right in the eye, and said, "Jackie, you seem to always have somebody who is out to get you. I think you need to start taking a look at yourself."

Wow, Mom! Bombs away! I was shocked by the accuracy, and thus pain, of her statement. I am blessed with a very fine relationship with my mother, and trust her absolutely, so I knew she wasn't simply out to get me. Her words prompted me to take a look at the *result* I was creating in my life. That result was victimhood. No matter what was going on, I always saw myself as the victim, always at the mercy of someone else, a someone else who took the form of antagonist in my life, there to deliver the painful message that I didn't fit in. I was simply recreating that experience of being the little girl on the bicycle who was convinced that the other girls were laughing at her and that she didn't fit in anywhere.

In other words, I was being right. I told myself over and over again that I didn't fit in, and I would either act in such a way on the job as to make sure that I didn't fit in, or I would find some authority figure with whom I could create enough friction to cause problems. I had to be right every single time about the fact that I didn't fit in, and I literally threw away job after job after job in order to make that statement absolutely true for myself. The beautiful part, from my unconscious point of view, was that none of these job failures was truly my fault. If I could point a finger at someone in the company who messed up my opportunities there, I got to say to myself, "Whew, it's not my fault--these things just happen to me...because I just don't fit in."

I always needed someone to blame for my failures. I was simply making myself right by consciously or subconsciously choosing to act in the manner where I didn't fit in. Then I would have to leave the job, and I could blame someone else for it. Once I saw this pattern, I became ready to let go of it. I wanted to take more responsibility for my life. The starkness of my mother's statement left me with no other choice. As they say in the movie Shawshank Redemption, "You've got to get busy living, or get busy dying." As long as I was continuing to fail in such an important area of my life, I was not living at all.

This actually brings up the very interesting question of success and failure. I was a failure in all these situations not because anyone else said I was, but because I *decided* I was. But the fact is that almost all successes and failures in life, with the possible exception of grades in school, are self-imposed and self-defined. That is, *we* decide what is a success and what is a failure. We might get fired from a job and consider that a failure. Well, what if we never wanted to be in that job in the first place? What if leaving that job frees us to do the very thing we have always wanted to do with our lives? Is it still a failure? I don't think so. Let me give you another way to look at this.

About twenty years ago, I was working as a secretary to an entertainment lawyer. Approximately six weeks after I started working for him, I would notice, every so often, that he would make me feel as if I was slow or incompetent. He would ask me why I didn't remember something he said he had absolutely told me earlier.

I started to question myself. I started to wonder if I was losing my memory, or really screwing up as much as he claimed. I was beginning to feel really bad about myself, and I feared making any more mistakes. Then on the night before Thanksgiving, when I was about to go home and prepare a dinner for my whole family, he told me I'd have to work late. I told him that was impossible, since I was in charge of our family dinner. He kept riding me to stay, and kept giving me more work, when I finally snapped. I told him, "I'm going home now...it's Thanksgiving."

He angrily responded, "No, you're not! If you do, don't bother coming in on Monday!"

I then responded, "Then I'll take my paycheck right now, because I'm not coming back!"

I remember what a miserable Thanksgiving that was for me, and, unfortunately, for the rest of my family. I cried all night, and felt very much like a failure for having lost my job in that manner.

Months later, I heard from another woman who also worked in his office. She told me that I had been his twentieth secretary in five years, and that he had later been caught using cocaine in his office!

Can you see that what sometimes looks like a failure isn't necessarily one? That it really was a very good thing for me to leave a job that was so abusive? Getting away from a person like that is a very good thing! We don't always--or even *often*--see these things right away, however.

Aside from grades and other *objective* measurements for evaluating people, most failure is self-imposed and self-defined! There is really no such thing as "failure" unless we choose to define something that way. And yet, we create failure, over and over, in our heads. We do so in order to live up to--or should I say, live down--to that negative belief about ourselves that we created somewhere in the past, about which we must absolutely be right.

....

Failure is self-imposed and self-defined.

....

Sometimes we say to ourselves something like this: "See, everything I do is a failure." We then live our lives around that basic organizing principle, that we fail at everything we try. And then every time something negative happens to us, we have an excuse. We can blame that unfortunate occurrence on the simple fact that we can't do anything right. In this way, we are continually locking in this definition of ourselves as a bumbling failure. Since we are defining ourselves, and since we have that obsessive need to be right, this method of living, left unchecked, will lead to real failure. We will have talked ourselves into screwing up everything of importance--love relationships, jobs, money, our body. This is all usually done subconsciously. Since we, and only we, have the power to define ourselves, and since we do have that need to be right, what we now want to do is to re-define ourselves...and be right in a more advantageous and useful way.

Exercise: *Rules*, or Things I'm Being *Right* About

What are *you* being right about in *your* own life? What are the rules by which you live your life? It's almost as though your mind runs on a software program that has certain rules built into it. Ask yourself now: What are those rules? What do you believe to be right in your own life? This is usually something dysfunctional. Take a few moments right now and look deep inside yourself, and see if you can discover those basic rules by which you live your life--the things about which you absolutely must be right, i.e. "I'll never lose weight," "I'll never be successful," "I'm the family 'screw-up,'" etc.

_____

_____

_____

_____

_____

_____

_____

_____

_____

_____

_____

If you're having trouble with this exercise, let me tell you the story of one of my clients, an architect named Sidney. When Sidney was ten years old, his grandfather was murdered in a holdup. His grandfather had recently become wealthy and had bought himself a beautiful new Cadillac a month before his untimely death. The ten-year-old Sidney watched these events take place and put together in his mind the belief that "If I get money and nice things, I will get killed because of them." This is simply how a ten-year-old mind puts things together. As you can imagine, Sidney led a life of self-impoverishment until he came to my office. I helped him recognize that he was sabotaging and limiting his income, and his joy in life, because he remained convinced, from the time he was ten years old, that having money and nice things would get him killed. This was all subconscious material until Sidney was willing to bring it up in therapy (that is, bring it up to the level of consciousness).

Sidney admitted that he had been totally unaware of the fact that these powerful thoughts governed his life. He realized that he had to be "right" about this belief, and since in his mind it was true, his only option was to keep himself from acquiring money and nice things in order to protect himself from his childhood fears. By first recognizing this belief about which he had to be right, and then by replacing it with a more positive view of the world, Sidney was able to release those old fears. Today he lives in a beautiful home, drives a nice car, and is able to enjoy the fruits of his architectural practice. You might want to look at your list of rules from the previous page and ask yourself: Are these rules that govern my life, these things about which I must be right, really keeping me from enjoying my life to the fullest?

Does telling the truth, or causing unconscious material to become conscious, make it disappear right away? Sometimes yes, but usually it takes a little time. With some difficult issues, it takes more time. But one usually feels a "lightening up" fairly quickly.

When you figure out what you're being right about, your next step is to turn that rightness around in the opposite direction. In my case, since I now realized that the long list of jobs from which I was fired was not due to the fault of others, but rather due to my own feelings of failure, which I unconsciously acted upon until I was fired, I could now create a new thing to be right about. I decided to start believing the following statement: "From now on, I am a success in every job I take on." (After all, I had years of trying it the other way!) With continued practice and time saying this new and positive commitment to myself, it became just as familiar as putting myself down had been in the past. In other words, I now told myself that I was going to be right about succeeding on the job instead of setting myself up to fail. What followed from that new conversation with myself was success, along with the startling realization that I am the constant creator of my own successes and my own life --and you are the constant creator of your life.

Here's a wonderful thing to know about success, failure, and being right...they are all almost always just perceptions! Ten people will have ten unique perceptions of one event. Who's right? Nobody...just perceptions. The reason you cannot go to a bookstore and find a book called "All the Ways to Fail" is because there is no such book. There is no way to define what failure really is, so why even have the word in your vocabulary? Since we're putting a label on everything, why not label things as *opportunities*, or *challenges*, and remove *failure*? A wonderful example: after Fred Astaire's first screen test, a 1933 memo from the MGM testing director said, "Can't act. Slightly bald. Can dance a little." Astaire kept that memo over the fireplace in his Beverly Hills home. Here's an even more remarkable example: the young Walt Disney was fired by a newspaper for lacking ideas. He also went bankrupt *several times* before he built Disneyland. If these men had *accepted* the notion of failure, and had then carried that failure story with them, can you see that they might have given up, rather than pushing forward to their goals?

....

Here's a wonderful thing to know about success, failure, and being right...they are all almost always just perceptions!

....

It's essential to look into your mind and find out what stories you carry with you. Those stories, or belief systems, might be keeping you from stepping out in life, taking risks, and feeling capable. They might have you feeling fear, resentment, an unhealthy level of competitiveness, and jealousy of others and their success. Okay, fine: you agree with me that you might have some negative programming, some stories that you tell yourself about which you have to be right. But how exactly do you go about digging them out?

There's a fairly easy way to do it. If you want to know what your stories are, look at the results in your life with which you're unhappy. For example, if you find that as soon as you lose weight, you seem to gain it back immediately, maybe deep down that's a validation of a story you carry called, "Everyone else can do it right but me...I Can Never Do Anything Right," or "I'll never be thin...I was born fat."

If that's what you find, then simply write yourself a new belief, a new internal rule by which to subconsciously organize and govern your life. It's really not that hard. In this case, you might write and then say to yourself, "My body supports me in every way, and consistently throws off excess weight." "I am a success at reaching and maintaining my natural body weight." "I *can* trust my body...just like when I was a kid."

Write those statements down, commit them to memory, write them on Post-it notes and put those notes in the bathroom, in the kitchen, in your bedroom, and in your office, and repeat those statements to yourself all day long. Whenever you have a free moment, tell yourself your new truths. When you are idling at a red light, remind yourself that you are a success at reaching and maintaining your natural body weight. When you are in the checkout line at the supermarket, instead of ogling all those sugary foods they keep up at the counter just to snare us when we're too hungry, remind yourself how easily you lose weight and how easily you keep it off. Tell yourself the new truths, and that way you can eventually stop believing in the old tapes you have been playing for yourself all these years.

Let's say your concern is not food, but instead has to do with jealousy. Let's say you find yourself feeling jealous all the time, a condition that many of my clients report. Perhaps you find yourself making up scenarios about your partner that don't exist. Let's assume that you want to break yourself of this habit. You may discover that the story or belief system inside you, the truth you've had to make right all this time, is "I'll never find a partner who won't cheat on me." Replace that love-destroying statement with a love-enhancing statement, such as this: "My mate loves me absolutely, and knows always how valuable our relationship is." Tell yourself a better truth and allow yourself to be right about that instead. Remember, *you're* making up this truth in your mind to begin with!

So the method I'm suggesting, once again, is simply to take a look at your life and focus on the results that you are getting that you do not like, whether they have to do with eating, relationships, money, work, or anything else. Chances are, behind any negative result in your life there is a negative story you're telling yourself, a negative belief, and you're making yourself be right about it, with negative results. Once you have found the result you don't like, and you can look back and identify the belief or truth underlying that result, simply write down for yourself that opposite truth, and start believing in it. This is about looking intensely inside yourself to see what you believe deep down, so that you can change those beliefs.

Does it matter how long you've had those beliefs? NO. Does it matter why you have these beliefs? NO. Does it matter where the belief came from? NO. Can anybody change his or her belief systems, even if that person has no prior experience of success? YES. Do other things effect our beliefs, like integrity and self-esteem? YES.

In other words, I do not believe it is necessary for you to sit and agonize over how that negative belief came into your life. Quite frankly, nobody cares. I'm not sure that there's anything useful in spending weeks or months agonizing on a therapist's couch as to how you got that belief. If anything, that sort of quest sounds to me very much like a search for guilty parties--in other words, it is a way to slough off personal responsibility. What matters here simply is this: that belief got in there somehow. We don't care how it got in. All we need to do now is replace it with a better belief.

I can put this another way. Let's say your child came home with a cold or the flu. What are you going to do--treat the symptoms, or sit there with the child for days, weeks or months, trying to figure out exactly which one of her little playmates gave her the illness? We both know that if we followed the latter course, our child would only get sicker. How a belief system sprung up is almost irrelevant. What matters is recognizing it, and replacing it with a more useful--and more fun--truth.

••

How a belief system sprung up is almost irrelevant. What matters is recognizing it, and replacing it with a more useful--and more fun--truth.

••

Chapter Eight -- Learning How to Talk to Yourself

The conversations we have with ourselves has everything to do with what happens in our life! Our conversations with ourselves, that is, our thoughts, spring from our belief systems-- that is, how we "hold" information. Here's how it works:

Early thoughts (i.e., "I don't fit in") lead to... ===>

(Self-created) Beliefs/stories (i.e., "I'm fat," "I'm different," "I'm ugly") lead to... ===>

**New conversations/thoughts   (i.e. "I hate my body," "I hate my face,"
"I hate my cellulite") lead to ===>**

Behavior (lying to feel important; eating too much) leads to ===>

Results (no friends; I get to be right about my belief that I don't fit in.)

To make it more simple, we can put this into four simple categories:

Thoughts (& Perceptions) ==> Beliefs ==> Behavior ==> Results

Let's take a look at the one of the most common dysfunctional beliefs we've heard... a person who tells herself or himself, "*I just have a slow metabolism.*"

Thought: *"Nothing works for me...I think I have a slow metabolism"*

Belief: *"I'll try this new Un-Diet, but it won't work for me, I'm different; my body is different."*

Behavior: Worried,   constantly   weighing   self; Deprivation...followed by overeating. Too many calories.

Results: *"See? I gained weight; nothing works for me; It's my metabolism."*

Can you identify in any way with this series of internal conversations?

We are constantly having a conversation with ourselves! Some call that conversation the "committee meeting," while some call it the "voice in our head." Even when we try to stop this voice, we are in fact having a conversation with it. The conversation goes on and on, hour after hour, day after day. Okay, what can we do about it? The conversations in your head cannot be stopped, but they can be directed. We can direct the conversation so that it actually turns into a productive discussion, instead of a destructive pattern of verbal abuse.

I'd like to share with you my personal experience with this problem...and the solution that worked for me. I have had a life-long problem with math. I have done work on myself regarding this issue, and remembered that my math problems started when I was ten years old, doing my math homework with my father at the kitchen table. My dad would get frustrated with me, and say "Jackie, don't you understand this?" What I *heard* him say was "How can you be so stupid?!" Ever notice how easy it is to make up that we're stupid?

I then began to erect a psychological wall called "I can't learn anything that has to do with numbers." Because of that wall, I would start out each evening feeling stupid and tortured by math. What followed this was a life-long battle with numbers and a terrible fear of being found out. I managed to somehow pass algebra and geometry, I believe, because of my personality and my teachers' sympathy over my earnest attempts to learn. But I always knew, deep down, that I was inept at math.

Then, at age 40, in graduate school I was required to take Statistics. I had a full-blown panic and eating attack when I saw the textbook. I knew that the teachers here were not going to care about how sweet I was. I got really scared, and found myself turning to food. I had learned to turn to food whenever I felt overwhelmed. This became my first attempt to change a long-time dysfunctional behavior. I knew I had to try something different and powerful, because all the evidence from my life showed me that I was about to have a serious problem with this statistics class. The first thing I did was ask myself what I was afraid of. The bottom-line fear was that I would fail at school. Then, I had to figure out the dysfunctional conversation (or belief system) that needed changing. I realized my nagging conversation was "You're stupid in math...you'll never pass this class."

I took three Post-it notes, and wrote the same message on all three, "You're brilliant with numbers". One was placed on my refrigerator, simply because it is a spot I often frequent. The second went up on my bathroom mirror because it is the first place I see in the morning when I brush my teeth. And the third was placed on my bedstand, because I know that the subconscious mind often works on the last thing it sees before sleep. The reason for choosing the word brilliant was because I knew I had to counteract 30 years of choosing the word stupid. We want to implant a strong enough belief to offset the original belief. Remember that the reason for creating a positive conversation first thing in the morning is because if you don't focus or implant something positive right away, your subconscious has a tendency to drift toward your fears. So now I have implanted a new thought for my subconscious to work on.

The result was subtle but amazing. A few weeks after doing this, I found myself standing in a line at my bank, balancing my checkbook...something I had never before been able to do. Suddenly my checkbook actually made sense to me! A simple thing like balancing was truly a miracle for me. It was also a tremendous feeling of freedom!

What are you going to write on your Post-It notes?

I want to emphasize for you that *there is nothing wrong with you* if your mind has the constant need to be right. There's a reason for that. The reason is not because you are sick, or crazy, or come from a dysfunctional whatever. The simple fact is that every human's subconscious mind has one greatest, most compelling need, and that is the need to be right. The mind seeks to be right...it works hard to be right...it always wants to be right! That's not just *your* mind. That's everybody's mind. I once read a story that said that we should think of the mind as an unruly puppy. If you try to take a stroll with a puppy, you'll find that he will first chase a squirrel until it runs up a tree. Then he'll jump after a bird, and then chase a lizard into a mud puddle, and as a result you might get your brand new shoes dirty.

What's the appropriate response or the solution? Telling the puppy not to chase squirrels and birds? Explaining to the puppy that he's the cause of your ruined shoes? Not very productive. The solution is to take responsibility by training the puppy to be obedient, one small step at a time. Puppies don't become obedient overnight, but we have to start somewhere--so we simply give that unruly puppy of a mind of ours better programming. Soon, it will behave the way we want it to. You can train your mind, taking small steps, to support you instead of undermine you. You can catch your unruly mind, as it drifts off toward negative thoughts, fears about the future, and bad experiences from the past, all of which keep you from being able to be present now. We actually can control our own thinking in this manner by identifying those negative beliefs and replacing them with positive statements about ourselves.

Let's take a look at this in a slightly different way. Suppose that I told you I was sending someone over to your house to live with you. He will dominate you, constantly criticize you, and will interrupt you every chance he gets. When you do something well, he will downplay it and find a way to criticize you anyway. When you fail at something, he'll be the first one to laugh at you, torment you, and humiliate you. When you choose to do the right thing, he will fill you with fear, anxiety and doubt and make you think that it was the wrong thing. No matter what you do, you will never win with this guy. What would you do if I said I was sending this person over to your house to live with you forever? You would say, "Hell, no! I won't live with him!" But you do live with him already. It's not a person, though. It's your own mind. Your mind criticizes you, tells you you're a failure, and interrupts any success thoughts with worries, fears, and anxiety.

If you were forced to live with or work with a pushy, despicable person like this, you would be ever-vigilant, ever-mindful that you were around someone who was out to get you, and therefore you'd be conscious about protecting yourself at all times. Then why are we not having the same self-protective relationship when it comes to our own minds? Because we are like fish who cannot see that they are in water. They can't see the water because they're *in* the water. Somehow we can't see what is right in front of us, because we've never seen anything different. We have somehow been tricked into believing that whatever our mind tells us is true! The mind has incessant conversations, all day long, but these are just conversations, not usually reality. In addition, since most of us have never learned how to *direct* our minds, those conversations are generally negative, eminating from our fears, rather than from our goals.

....

We have somehow been tricked into believing that whatever our mind tells us is true!

....

Since the mind seeks to be right, it is always looking for someone to blame. We're not really examining our lives and our selves. If we did, we'd see that life presents itself to us on a platter from which we may freely select what we experience. Nothing is forced upon us except that which our mind chooses to grab onto. We've been deceived into thinking that what we experience and feel is caused by forces outside of us. Whenever something happens that makes us feel uncomfortable, we instinctively turn to blame something or someone else for what just happened. Because of this tendency, we've never come to understand that only by taking responsibility can we move forward through anything and everything in life.

Can anyone really make you angry? The surprising answer is no. Instead, we become angry as a result of the external stimulus we have just experienced and the meaning (or belief systems) we attach to that. The fact is, however, that we do not have to become angry just because someone does or says something provocative. Like forgiveness, anger is a choice. It is *not* an automatic response.

···

Like forgiveness, anger is a choice. It is *not* an automatic response.

···

Is there anything in your life in the past that used to trigger an angry response in you that today you take in stride? If that's the case, then you have clear evidence that anger is in fact a choice. You chose to become angry in the past at that particular kind of event, and today you choose not to be angry. The great news is that you can transfer this decision-making power to virtually everything that comes along in your life. If you believe that someone can make you angry, you'll be getting angry all the time! That alone puts you at the *effect* of life, rather than *creating your life*. Remember, responsibility is not blame. It is simply ownership of thoughts and actions.

To sum up, we cannot stop the chatterbox in our mind, but we can redirect it. The first step in changing a dysfunctional behavior is to recognize that it is dysfunctional or non-productive, and that it comes from an internal conversation. Believe it or not, this is a difficult step for many people. Most people, even if they accept this concept, would still say things like, "Yeah, I believe that to be true, but not for me--I'm different! I'll never be able to do math, to keep weight off, to trust a partner in a love relationship. I never have, and I never will!" Most people don't believe that they can change the conversation they have with themselves and thus change their lives. They believe that it might be possible for others, but not for them. This, too, of course, is a negative conversation that these people are having in their minds. And they could change the course of their thinking if they want to. Do you?

Whatever you create in your mind about a particular situation, you'll find you're usually right! So the place to start your Un-Diet isn't at the refrigerator or the supermarket check-out stand. It's in your mind!

The Bottom Line on Right and Wrong

I'd like to discuss with you the true relationship between *perceptions* and the concept of *right and wrong.*

You've got the Ten Commandments--don't cheat, don't steal, don't murder, and so on. You've got the laws of the United States of America--don't cheat on your taxes, don't run a red light, don't yell fire in a crowded movie theater if there is no fire, and so on. But once you get past our basic sense of what is morally acceptable and the laws that any society needs in order to govern itself and avoid chaos, there really is no right and wrong! I'll say it again, because it's so important. **Once you get past the societal laws and moral imperatives, there really is no right and wrong!**

Rather, there is a whole bunch of opinions and perceptions. Everyone has opinions and beliefs--and everyone is right about his or her own feelings and perceptions.

One of the worst things we can do to another person is tell that person that she is wrong about the way she feels. It ought to be a crime to tell someone that he has no right to be sad, that he should "snap out of it," that she couldn't possibly be hungry because she just ate four hours ago, that he has no right to feel the way he feels. We are all entitled to our perceptions, and though they may not always be accurate reflections of the world around us, they are our perceptions about the world, and therefore they should not be criticized. Our perceptions are what's real for us. No one else has a right to tell us what's real for us. What a wonderful world it would be if everyone could understand and accept this!

The problem begins when we believe that we have a right to judge other people's perceptions--or when other people believe they have a right to judge ours. Trouble also comes when it becomes important, or even urgent, that we make other people agree with our perception or opinion. Once we try to impose our worldview on others, it will become extremely important for us to always be right all the time! It is virtually impossible to have a healthy relationship, or any relationship at all, with a person who needs to be right all the time.

115

If you can accept the idea that others may disagree with you and your relationship with them can remain completely intact nonetheless, then you have a solid relationship with that person. A relationship can thrive and flourish when two people understand that it's okay to disagree and discuss. If, on the other hand, you have a relationship where one of you always needs to be right, as we discussed earlier, this relationship will be draining, unhappy, and fraught with conflict.

When you find yourself needing to win a conversation, you'll see that you feel tight, tense, and defensive. When we can give up the need to be right, we can relax--physically and emotionally. We can let go of fighting and move on. We can also take in new information. We can accept new ideas from other people. We can even take in whole new perceptions, any time we want, without feeling guilty about giving up an old belief. We can thus make new brain connections more often. Let me give you an example from my own life.

One night, my husband and I were coming home from a party, and I was doing the driving. My husband began to criticize my driving--at least that's how it felt to me. I remember feeling myself tense up, in physical readiness for defending myself and attacking back. Then suddenly he said to me, "You know, I am so tense when you tailgate the car in front of you, that I really can't enjoy the drive!"

I was about to defend myself, when suddenly I stopped and thought about what he just said to me. I realized that he said he couldn't enjoy driving with me! That's not what I want to have with my husband. Suddenly I found myself telling him I didn't want that. I wanted him to enjoy every minute in the car when we were together. Then I told him I would stop tailgating immediately, and I did so. It wasn't that he was *right*--what one perceives as too close may not be the same for someone else. But when I looked at it from his point of view, I could understand his feelings and his perceptions. This is not at all about giving up or surrendering in the battle of the sexes. This was about gaining something--the ability to let go of a need to be right! What a gift when we can do that! Now, when I drive somewhere with my husband, he has fun, and so do I. And so does the driver ahead of me, who no longer has somebody tailgating him for miles down the freeway.

The lesson here for me was that my perceptions were different from my husband's. In my mind, I had been driving safely all the time. That was my perception of my driving. His perception was different. Because I was able to hear his perspective without the need to fight back, I was able to make an adjustment that definitely improved the state of our marriage. My decision to change doesn't mean I was wrong. It means instead that I'm changing because the new approach works better for me, for my mate, and for our partnership.

....

Because I was able to hear his perspective without the need to fight back, I was able to make an adjustment that definitely improved the state of our marriage.

....

There's a famous line from the movie Cool Hand Luke: "What we have here is a failure to communicate." Here's another example of how undelivered communications can kill relationships.

Marcie and Fred are clients of mine who have been married for twenty years. Both are journalists, so communication is what their professional lives are all about. They were not quite as successful at communicating at home, however.

In our first session, Marcie told me that Fred was always making them late for their appointments. It seemed to Marcie that Fred would wait too long before getting ready to leave, and then the rush would start--with angry words ensuing. I asked Marcie what she had communicated to Fred about all this. She said she told him that he should be more careful to allow himself a more realistic amount of time. That way he could keep his word without feeling rushed.

I asked Fred how he felt when Marcie told him all this. He said that his first reaction was defensiveness, and then he explained why he needed extra time. Marcie then said that Fred had found a way to blame the whole thing on her.

With most couples, the conversation usually ends here, with both people feeling angry and incomplete. I was very proud of Fred and Marcie, who were willing to come in and talk to me about an issue that could have appeared to be trivial. The issue, however, was not really about lateness. It was more about communication and the need to make the other partner wrong.

I suggested that the two of them find a solution where neither of them had to be wrong. The solution that they came up with was this: Marcie would mark their home calendar with their appointments. Each of them would agree to be ready fifteen minutes early for all appointments. That agreement involved both of them. This way, they would create some cushioning for unexpected delays. At their next session a month later, they reported back to me that the solution was working. Incidentally, they arrived on time.

The most difficult part for most couples is to stop needing to be right. Once we give up that need to be right, and we do that by discovering what it is that we need to be right about, we can then find a solution to the problem. When you come up with solutions, the original complaints generally disappear. The only reason that most people don't want to make this happen is because it's more important for them to make their partner wrong! In this scenario, Marcie gave up her need to make Fred wrong for their lateness, taking personal responsibility instead by coming up with an excellent solution to the problem.

Don't let anyone tell you this process is easy. It's very hard to communicate our deepest needs and fears to anyone, especially to our partner or spouse. But the rewards are so magnificent. As a result of working through this difficulty, Marcie and Fred reported that they both felt complete, closer than ever before, and even more loving and intimate. It is impossible to stay angry with someone who takes responsibility. If you want to diminish the amount of anger that other people hold toward you, take even more responsibility in your current life for your actions--stop making others wrong--and watch the magic happen.

....

If you want to diminish the amount of anger that other people hold toward you, take even more responsibility in your current life for your actions--stop making others wrong--and watch the magic happen.

....

What about you? Do you have perceptions or concepts about the world that you have enshrined and placed on the same level as the Ten Commandments or the U.S. Constitution? It's quite possible that you do, because we all do. It's human nature. The human mind has a powerful need to be right. The question we have to ask ourselves, though, is what price are we paying for our intense need to be right? What's the emotional cost? What's the cost to all of our relationships?

Exercise:

Take some time right now and ask yourself about the last three times that you got into conflict with another human being. Try to remember exactly what was going on, what you felt. Ask yourself in each of those cases whether the situation might have gone differently had you not felt the need to defend your perception of the world at all costs, if that, in fact, happened. What about the other person? Were you truly able to listen to the other person's perception of the situation, especially if his or her perception was radically different from your own?

Conflict   **About What Did I Need To Be Right?**

_____

_____

_____

_____

_____

I'd like you to promise me that the next time someone offers you a perception of a situation that's different from yours, you will be open to hearing that differing perception without the need to get defensive and stand up for your own view of the world. This doesn't mean that you have to be a doormat and simply accept other people's perceptions as being appropriate for you. All I'm asking is that you consider the fact that other people might see a situation differently from the way we do. Their worldview, even though it may conflict with our own, is worth hearing and understanding, because through listening, truly listening, we show love.

Chapter Nine -- Think Thin -- The Psychology of Permanent Weight Loss

I recently went back to Florida for my thirtieth high school reunion. From the moment I checked into the hotel in Miami, I felt fatter than I'd ever felt before. I thought I could see my thighs gaining inches and cellulite right in front of my eyes. I was certain that I would not fit into the dress I was planning to wear for the reunion. These feelings were strikingly familiar. They were the same exact feelings I had over thirty years ago when I first attended this high school. Those feelings, in fact, lasted until my return home. While I was unpacking my bags, I suddenly felt thin again...as if I'd just lost twenty pounds!

Given that I've done years and years of psychotherapy on myself, I found it incredible that a reunion could suck me back into my high school feelings of inadequacy, and bring me back to a time when I hated my body and felt fat. And yet--the feelings I felt now as an adult were just as intense as the original feelings I felt back when I was a teenager. It's amazing how the mind pulls forth old, unfinished business for us to see. Even though these old feelings make us feel terrible in the present moment, they are actually a *gift*...a signal of what still needs attention or completion.

In just an instant, a sight, a feeling, or even a smell can trigger us to feel feelings that have nothing to do with what's going on in the present moment. It is important to understand how negative thinking and pessimism work on our minds to create negative, repetitive patterns in the brain. Scientists have now learned that the more we exercise the brain, the stronger it gets--just like any other muscle. Also, the more connections our brains develop, through complex psychological thinking, reading books, taking classes, and other means, the more the brain actually weighs--it literally gets heavier with use.

Studies show that when people listen to simple and repetitive music, the firing of neurons in their brain tends to be simple and repetitive. In contrast, when people are exposed to Mozart and complex varied musical connections, the firing of neurons in their brain tends to be more varied and complex, leading to more brain connections. Whenever we learn something new, our brain makes a new connection. (I hope that's happening for you as you read this book.) When we stop learning, however, our brain begins to disconnect from itself. In addition, we have now seen that the more a person continues to learn and grow, the more connective tissue actually grows in the brain. That tissue can be observed through MRI exams. This means you can actually create more connections or growth in your own brain by the *way* you think.

··

You can actually create more connections or growth in your own brain by the *way* you think.

··

Please don't be alarmed, however, if you're worried that thinking too much is going to put excess pounds on your brain. I guarantee that all the thinking in the world will not create the slightest ripple on your bathroom scale, which I hope you've thrown out by now anyway!

Let's take an example from real life that may help us to understand this concept better. When we drive from point A to point B and take the same route over and over again, we have a tendency to want to travel that road every single time, because it becomes so familiar. It is the same with our mind. When we think the same thoughts over and over again, no matter where they came from, we then have a tendency to go to those same thoughts--even if those thoughts are dysfunctional and get in the way of having a better life.

We stay with those thoughts because those thoughts are what we know, what we are familiar with, what feels comfortable to us. This helps to explain why battered women will stay with their abusive husbands. It's what they know. It doesn't matter to the mind that this is an abominable situation. What matters to the mind is to avoid pain. In many, many people, the worst pain possible is the fear associated with change. The pain associated with change can be even more fearful to the human mind than the physical pain that comes from assault. People would rather continue to receive the pain they know than to go into the unknown!

Let's talk about food. When we believe we are fat, it doesn't matter what the scale or the mirror says. It doesn't matter what our family, friends or doctor might say. It doesn't matter what we do or how much weight we lose--we are fat in our mind, and the mind always wins. Once we believe that we are fat, this belief then gains momentum and validation. We might sit with certain people at work and grumble about having gained a few pounds. These people, who probably don't like their bodies either, will sympathize and lock in those feelings for you. So we build what are called neuro-pathways in the brain, or well-traveled pathways of thinking.

As we've discussed, popular culture doesn't help. Advertisers of all kinds...sellers of cosmetics, weight loss systems, jewelry, and clothing, to name a few...seek to brainwash us into believing that we're not okay the way we are. Ads stimulate a sense of discomfort or dis-ease with our current appearance, surroundings, and possessions. We are bombarded thousands of times a day with messages that emphasize just how unfit we are to function in the world or attract and keep a mate. Negative thinking is enforced every time we turn on the radio or TV.

Let's take a closer look at those neuro-pathways in the brain and how they function. If we have always been fearful, especially of failure, then when we are presented with, let's say, an opportunity for a job promotion, we will immediately go to that well-traveled pathway of "uh-oh, what if I can't do the job?" This mental reaction could stop us from accepting such a promotion, because we figure we're safe where we are now. The safety of what we know becomes our well-traveled neuropathway, and we continue traveling it throughout our life, even though inside we may hate ourselves, over and over again, for being so fearful.

We continue traveling those well-traveled neuropathways throughout our life, even though inside we may hate ourselves, over and over again, for being so fearful.

Now let's see how these brain connections and pathways work in terms of pessimism and optimism. A pessimist, usually very early on in life, starts making brain connections that tend toward the negative. A child might say, "I probably won't get picked for that team...nobody likes me." This then becomes the pattern that he tells himself as his life continues. "See?" he'll say as the years go by. "I never seem to fit in anywhere." That sense of "nobody likes me" becomes the thing he's right about. It becomes a well-traveled, repetitive connection or automatic negative thought. It's subtle. We don't realize we've created it. It's not as though there's some big neon sign in our brain that says, "Attention! Warning! You have just created a negative thought which you are likely to repeat for the rest of your life!" No, alas, there is no such signal. We have no idea that we have created this pessimistic mindset. It simply feels like a fact...based on all of our experiences. We don't see that we've actually created the problem through our own thinking.

We don't see that we've actually created the problem through our own thinking.

Remember my story of being four years old when I first experienced the feeling of not fitting in, and feeling fat? This became my repetitive feeling pattern, my well-traveled pathway, where I always went in my mind, even thirty years later. The thirtieth reunion simply triggered a decades-old feeling of not fitting in and feeling fat. You might think that since I'm an expert in these matters, I might be immune to this sort of thinking. I wish that were the case! I've got to do the same work in this area as everybody else in order to feel secure in myself. This is why we must all learn how to re-program our mind. If we don't re-program ourselves, we will be hopelessly at the mercy of old, outdated and completely dysfunctional tapes that play over and over again in our mind.

Pessimists like to call themselves realists. They don't think they're being pessimistic at all, but rather feel that they are simply facing reality--and they always imply that you are not facing reality if you don't think like them. If you aren't suffering, you're not dealing in the real world. You're a Pollyana. That's the battle cry of the pessimist. Let's take a look at some of the major differences between pessimists and optimists.

Pessimists consistently blame others, and always see themselves as a victim. Optimists, on the other hand, take complete responsibility for their behavior and the results they achieve. If they don't like what they've created, they take responsibility for fixing it or dealing with it.

Pessimists focus on problems, while optimists focus on solutions.

Pessimists focus on what they don't want, while optimists focus on what they do want.

Pessimists always notice what's missing. Optimists see what's right, and congratulate themselves every small step of the way...because that motivates them and gets them through the obstacles and tough times.

Pessimists stay stuck in the drama of what they *perceive* to be rejections. Optimists observe obstacles, and focus immediately on how to overcome them.

Pessimists believe that they must fight their way through life and the problems life throws at them. Optimists, on the other hand, create a vision for what they want, and then take responsibility for the game of making it come true. They don't wait for life to happen. They make life happen.

Pessimists count problems, while optimists count blessings.

Pessimists come across to others as angry, needy, chronic complainers or victims. Optimists come across as successful and self-assured.

Pessimists worry constantly about the future and about what might happen. Optimists are excited about future possibilities.

Why is this important? As we continue with our patterns of negative thinking, we drive away from us healthy thinkers, because healthy thinkers are repelled by the truly unattractive pattern of negative thinking that we might display. If we want to be attractive to healthy people, we have to change. More important, if we don't change, we will have set up a continual pattern of floating subconsciously to the negative, fearful, or worried side of everything! So the negative behavior flourishes and feeds on itself, until it becomes a self-fulfilling prophecy, and we get to be right about how pathetic we are. It's important to see how negativity leads us automatically to feeling bad about ourselves--and it definitely affects our health...in too many ways to mention! Pessimists never realize that their *thinking* is faulty. They feel that their thinking is a natural and correct response to the way life treats them.

....

Our thinking naturally moves us in the direction of our goals. If we do not consciously choose goals, then our thinking usually moves us in the direction of our fears. The only thing bigger than fear is intention. This means that when we set an intention or goal, we have now taken any fear that we might naturally drift toward and we have replaced it with something far more powerful. Creating intention, or setting a goal, is the most important thing we can do to combat our fear, once we have created fear.

....

We need to see that we either program ourselves to succeed, or we let life and other people program us to fail. We are going to get programmed one way or another. The only question is by whom and the nature of the programming that we are going to experience. Whether that programming is functional or dysfunctional is really is up to us.

Our conscious mind programs our subconscious mind, in the same way that a computer is programmed. If you put garbage, or negative thoughts into your computer, garbage or negativity will come out of it! So if we believe (or program our computer to believe) that we are fat, unattractive, and different, we will end up feeling that way all the time.

When we start to have hopeful, positive thoughts, the brain works better. It makes better connections. We feel more relaxed, which leads to much better productivity, which leads to better results, which leads to feeling better about ourselves, and so on. We have left a vicious cycle to enter into a gaining cycle. And I'm not talking about weight gain. I'm talking about gaining self-esteem.

It is vital that we learn how to re-program ourselves. Let's take some time now to re-program our thinking and attitudes using the following tools:

Tools for changing belief systems

1) First and most important, you must really *want* to change the patterns in your life.

2) Discover your faulty belief systems by working backwards--ask yourself what results in your life are you getting that you don't like. Then ask yourself what you must be telling yourself, believing, making yourself right about, that is leading to this result.

3) Write down the actual negative statement that you have been telling yourself all this time.

4) Write down the opposite belief. Create a new belief that will drown out the old one. Always state that new belief in a positive form. (This way, you shift from being a victim to taking some kind of control...any control in your life. You're finding a way to take responsibility for, or control of, the solution.)

Here are some examples of how to do this. We might look at the results we are currently obtaining in our lives and say, "I never have enough money, and my debt's too high." We might then realize the actual negative belief we've been telling ourselves is this: "I'll never have money...I'll never be successful." So we now write down the *opposite* belief: "I create abundance in every aspect of my life."

Let's try another example, this time with food. The result we're currently experiencing is excess weight. So we analyze that result and determine the belief that *creates* that result. That negative belief says, "Nothing works...I'll never be thin." So we develop and write down the *opposite* belief (so as to create the *opposite* result). That might be: "My body seeks and stays at its natural and comfortable weight."

5) Write the new belief on two or three Post-It notes, and place them in strategic spots you're guaranteed to see every day.

6) Look at that new belief, envision it in your mind, and repeat it to yourself every morning upon waking and every evening before sleep. Be sure to notice the remarks your inner critic makes every time you state your new belief. Those remarks should shift, usually in subtle ways, in a fairly short amount of time.

7) Each day, create a little more belief in that statement. Perhaps you can take an action that would show that you are actually beginning to believe in that new statement.

8) As soon as the first sign of something new appears in your life, acknowledge yourself profusely. Buy yourself a present, do something special for yourself, reward yourself for having created something better in your life. It will never *seem* like you created it...and will always appear like an accident or a mistake.

9) Do this vigilantly for a full month.

10) After that month is over, and you see results--even if they're small--keep going. Keep on re-telling yourself that new belief...for the rest of your life, if necessary.

You will probably laugh the first time you speak your new belief to yourself. You'll probably not believe it. Keep it up anyway! I know you've had much more practice believing you're not capable or successful. But now is the time to try this new approach, and you will see just how productive it will be for you! It takes time to substitute the new belief. Remember, though, that we are always having a conversation with ourselves, so we might as well make it worthwhile.

....

We are always having a conversation with ourselves, so we might as well make it worthwhile.

....

Again, it doesn't matter where that original negative conversation started or why. Insight is sometimes helpful. It is interesting and it can even provide a jolt of self-understanding. But remember: insight doesn't produce change. Only ACTION produces change! All the powerful insight in the world doesn't change anything. But a decision to change, a promise, a commitment--that's powerful and that can and will produce change in your life.

What stories do you tell yourself about your weight? About your body? About your ability to be healthy and fit? Do you tell yourself, "I'll never be slim...nobody in my family is." Do you tell yourself that you have bad genetics, or no self-control? Whatever those stories are that you tell yourself, it's time to give yourself some positive messages. These include: "I can be slim because I'm committed to my health," "I'm the one in this family who wins the battle against weight," or "I can stay connected to my hunger and honor my body."

When you tell yourself these new truths, and you allow yourself to be right about being successful, a whole new exciting world will open up for you, and you are going to want to revitalize every single aspect of your life!

Chapter Ten -- It's Better To Talk About It Than Eat Over It

No one ever said marriage would be easy. Without workable communication skills, marriage, and virtually every other human relationship, is doomed to struggle and failure. So often when I work with married couples, I see the individuals slowly getting angrier and angrier because they are not communicating their desires. Instead, they feel resentful that their mates don't know what they want and don't automatically give them what they want! Many of us have expectations that set us up for constant disappointment. Those expectations are based on the fact that we really believe that everybody else should think exactly the way we do!

....

We really believe that everybody else should think exactly the way we do!

....

We say things to ourselves like, "If he really loved me, he would have done it differently!" This is self-centered, and, more important, very foolish behavior. If you are an adult, nobody has been put here on this planet to attend to your needs. That includes your spouse, your partner, your parents, and especially your children. Instead of expecting things from others, if we want to be happy, we must learn how to ask for what we want...with the full understanding, tolerance, and respect for the fact that we may hear the word "no." As the Rolling Stones say, "You can't always get what you want."

If you can replace your expectations of other people and their behavior with an ability to make requests of others, secure in the knowledge that you may or may not get that request met, but that your life will go on either way, you are on your way to a happy marriage, or a happy relationship with any human being you encounter. Let me give you an example of how I had to learn this for myself.

For the first five years of my marriage, whenever I did my own laundry, I would pick up my husband's laundry from his closet and do it at the same time. I just figured it was easier to make a full load of whites and a full load of colors. As the years passed, when I got much busier in my own work, I noticed that my husband was doing his laundry...but he never picked up mine!

I started to get secretly angry with him. I didn't say anything, but I kept on noticing this behavior, which struck me as unfair and thoughtless. One day, I blew my top and I read him the riot act about how selfish he was for never thinking of doing my laundry with his. He was quite shocked by my outburst. His response was quite innocent. He said that he was never sure of which things would run or shrink in the laundry, and he was afraid to ruin something of mine. It turned out that he wasn't being purposely selfish, as I thought. Also, he never *asked* me to do his laundry. My assumption, that he would do something for me simply because I did it for him, was a silly one, and actually a rather destructive one in terms of our entire relationship. It was destructive because it was a "private expectation" rather than an "expressed request."

....

My assumption, that he would do something for me simply because I did it for him, was a silly one, and actually a rather destructive one in terms of our entire relationship. It was destructive because it was a "private expectation" rather than an "expressed request."

....

If I want my husband to do my laundry, what I need to do is make a request of him, instead of expecting it. Many people have a hard time with this life lesson--I certainly did, at least at first. The rule of thumb is this: expectations always set us up for disappointment and upset down the road. An expectation is a preconceived resentment waiting to happen. Expectations need to be replaced with requests and agreements.

When we expect that other people will read our minds and know exactly what we want, even if we do not ask directly for it, we set ourselves up for enormous disappointments, resentments and anger. Let me share with you another story from my own personal experience. One night, around eleven p.m., I felt myself stricken with some sort of nausea and diarrhea. I went to the bathroom to find some medication, because I knew, or at least I thought I knew, that there was some left. It was gone--it turned out that my husband had taken the last of it earlier that day.

Distressed, I said to my husband, who was watching a TV show, "Omigod...there are no pills left. It's eleven o'clock at night--I'll have to go to the drugstore and get more!" His response, as he still watched TV, was this: "I'll see you when you get back!"

All I can remember about that ride to the all-night drugstore was that I had never been that angry in my whole life. I remember I could hardly keep my foot on the accelerator because my whole body was shaking so badly. Then suddenly I realized that I had expected my husband to leap gallantly into the air and say, "That's okay, honey! I'll go to the drugstore and get you the pills! You wait here!"

The fact is that my husband is a very good guy, and if I had asked him to do so, he probably would have done it. The truth was that I was hoping to manipulate him into going out to the drugstore without my having to ask. I thought that the mere idea of me going off at eleven o'clock at night to the drugstore, would've been enough to galvanize my husband and get him to run out the door. Have you ever done that? Have you ever hoped to plant a seed in someone else's mind, instead of directly requesting what you want that person to do?

....

Have you ever hoped to plant a seed in someone else's mind, instead of directly requesting what you want that person to do?

....

It's fairly common behavior, but it's self-defeating. As much as I might hate to admit it, my husband was not put on earth to meet all of my needs. He has his own life, his own responsibilities, and his own needs (and by the way, I'm not here to meet all of *his* needs either!). If we want people to do things for us, we have to ask them directly. If we are merely trying to plant a seed in their minds about what we want them to do for us, we are guilty of trying to manipulate them. There are two outcomes to manipulation, and both of them are bad. The first is that the manipulation will succeed. This will invariably cause the other person to resent us, even as they go about our bidding. The second possibility is that the manipulation will fail, in which case we will resent them. We'll tell ourselves things like, "He knew exactly what I meant when I said, 'We're out of pills, and I have to go to the drugstore.' He knew exactly what I had in mind, and he didn't do it any way!"

That's very angry thinking. That's why I say that anger is frequently about expectations--and expectations often have to do with manipulation and expecting that the other person will read our mind and do whatever they find in our mind that we want them to do for us. That's just not how the world works.

How do we get out of this conundrum?

Here are the three keys to resolving interpersonal conflicts:

1) *Find* a way to take responsibility for your upset. I have emphasized the word *find* because it is extremely difficult to look at ourselves when we are angry at others...especially when we are really angry. I found a way to take responsibility for my upset when I realized that I didn't ask him for what I really wanted. Instead, I expected him to know.

2) Communicate your newly understood sense of responsibility to the other person. In this case, I told my husband that I realized I was trying to manipulate him and was hoping he would read my mind.

3) Take action that changes the way you will react in the future. Here, I committed to my partner that I will surrender all my expectations and instead will ask directly for what I want. (Always remember when making a request that you must be willing to hear "No.")

By the way, when I came home from the drugstore, I had calmed down considerably, which is what happens when you take responsibility. I told my husband exactly what had gone on in my mind. His response: he felt upset with himself for not having realized that he could have gone out and gotten those pills for me. He said he felt embarrassed by the fact that he did not rise to the occasion for me, even though I didn't directly express what I wanted. As he put it, "And I'm a jerk." We both felt that we learned something that night and we grew closer. So the lesson here is that anger and expectations are tied together deeply, and by reducing our expectations of other people, we can reduce the amount of anger we experience in our lives. When we reduce our anger, we also reduce our need to stuff our feelings with food.

....

Anger and expectations are tied together deeply, and by reducing our expectations of other people, we can reduce the amount of anger we experience in our lives.

....

Learning the basics of communication skills is the easiest way to have it all. In terms of food, the ability to communicate with loved ones is vital. What we don't express, we suppress. What we suppress, we eat over. It's that simple. When we possess great communication skills, our self-esteem goes up, because when we feel really confident within ourselves, we find it easier to trust and express our feelings and our intuition. Another reason why self-esteem is so tied to communications skills is that self-esteem allows us to really speak our mind, even in the face of disagreement and rejection. It comes from knowing that our thoughts and feelings are valid and worthwhile regardless of whether the other person agrees with us or not.

Communication and self-esteem, therefore, form a basic foundation for learning how to set boundaries with other people. **We need to learn how to set boundaries in our life.** If we don't, people will eventually step all over us, and we will end up feeling victimized over and over, not realizing that we created the problem ourselves by our lack of boundaries. I remember feeling sad and disillusioned when I learned, in one of my psychology classes, that most human beings have a natural inclination to take advantage of other people. Instead of being upset over this, or being afraid of this happening, however, we must understand that we teach people how to treat us by the way we set or don't set boundaries with them.

....

We teach people how to treat us by the way we set or don't set boundaries with them.

....

If one of your recurring conversations with yourself is, "Why do these things always happen to me?", it's very possible that you have a problem with setting boundaries. Here are some examples of boundaries that you can lovingly set with your spouse, significant other, best friend, parent, or child, simply by making requests, in a calm and composed fashion. (By the way, failing to make such boundaries always leads to regret.)

With your spouse:

1) Don't put me down in public.

2) Don't flirt with the opposite sex.

3) Don't cheat on me in any way.

4) Don't be late without calling.

5) Don't gamble away our money.

6) Don't take drugs.

7) Respect my opinion as much as you respect your own.

8) Please honor my relationship with my family and get along.

9) Please clean up after yourself.

10) Respect my belongings.

11) Don't yell or strike out physically.

You can decide on the appropriate boundaries to set with your spouse. What do you need in your life? In your marriage or relationship? These are the things that you have every right to ask for. If your spouse or partner is unwilling or unable to live up to the requests that you make, you have to then take responsibility for the fact that you don't have to continue your relationship with that person, if doing so compromises your basic value system too severely. You always have choices, whether or not you want to take responsibility for them.

With children, common boundaries that successful parents set include the following:

1) Don't talk back.

2) Don't join a gang.

3) Don't steal...ask me for what you want.

4) Don't stay out all night--you must be home by a certain time.

5) Don't take drugs

6) Don't yell or strike out physically

7) Respect our belongings

If you don't have agreements and boundaries in your relationships, you are setting yourself up for massive upsets down the road. It is extremely freeing to have a clear understanding in your relationships of what is and what isn't acceptable to both of you.

It is extremely freeing to have a clear understanding in your relationships of what is and what isn't acceptable to both of you.

The most important thing to know about requests is *that we should not make them when we are angry.* Also, we don't want to make them out of need. We want to make requests as a result of wants. When we make requests, they need to be solution-oriented, and conveyed lovingly. In the workplace, requests need to be made in a professional and caring manner. Of course, the question that arises is this: "What happens if I make requests and my partner keeps saying no?" If this is happening, you need to question *why* you are in that relationship. Then, if you still want to remain in the relationship, you'd better be willing to get professional help, or you are doomed to a life of misery. Without agreements, requests, promises, and trust, you don't have a relationship--you have a dictatorship!

Without agreements, requests, promises, and trust, you don't have a relationship--you have a dictatorship!

Let's talk now about *the three basic problems in communication* that affect most relationships. How important is it to address these problems? Let's face it: life is about relationships with other people. These relationships may be long-term, like family or marriage ties, or they may be of shorter duration, like our bonds to the people in our workplace. Or they may be fleetingly brief: a conversation with a stranger; a purchase in a department store; even a glance at another driver on the road. But when you stop and think about it, relationships with other people really *define* the quality of our lives.

Relationships with other people really *define* the quality of our lives.

In fact, when we reach the end of our lives, what do we really look back upon? Not our weight, or our car, or how much money we have in the bank. At the end of our lives, we look back at the relationships we had with family members, friends, spouses, partners...it's the people and how we got along with them that truly matters the most.

We don't have to wait for old age or death to discover the power of relationships to determine the quality of our lives, however. If we have a fight in the morning with our spouse or partner, we will carry that upset with us for the rest of the day. Every time we have an interaction that we feel bad about, we bear that unhappiness for hours ... days... weeks...or even longer. How well does *your* day go when you have a fight with your mate? Now multiply that sense of discomfort by all the people you're going to meet today. What you end up with is a widening circle of pain. Great communication skills can avert most negative interactions...before they even begin. You may not always see eye-to-eye with your significant other, parent, child, boss, customer, or client, but at least you can communicate better with that person and thus avoid the misery and pain that poor communication guarantees. The great news is that these three basic problems in communication can easily be solved with the techniques I will share with you.

The first problem in communication is the inability to remove make-wrongs. A "make-wrong" is a way of expressing ourselves that, simply put, makes the other person wrong. When we begin a statement with "You always" or "You never remember" or any words that take as their starting point the fact that we're right and the other person is wrong, what do we get? We get defensiveness. It's virtually guaranteed. If Sam tells Samantha she always burns the toast, Samantha will naturally respond in a defensive manner. She'll feel the need to justify her behavior, *even if what Sam said isn't true.* The person we make wrong will invariably *react* to our statement, rather than respond to it...and that guarantees an argument, bad feelings, and a definite downward bump in the quality of the relationship.

So why do we do it? Why do we feel the need so often to make someone else wrong? Because when we make someone else wrong, we then get to be right. And feeling right just seems to feel so good--even though the hidden cost is that the relationship always suffers.

....

Feeling right just seems to feel so good--even though the hidden cost is that the relationship always suffers.

....

How do you remove the make-wrongs from your communication with others? Very simply, by taking responsibility. If you take responsibility for a situation, it's impossible to make someone else wrong. Taking responsibility relieves everyone else because now you, yourself can fix whatever the problem is. Let me give you an example of how my own negativity in a situation forced me to take responsibility for a problem.

In New York City, it's fairly common to walk for blocks with the same handful of strangers. You're going at about the same pace. You end up waiting at the same corners for lights to change. You probably won't talk to them--it *is* New York, after all--but you're sort of in the same posse as you head to your destination.

One time, my husband and I were walking down Broadway in Manhattan when I thought I noticed my husband ogling one of the people walking in our group, a young woman wearing very high heels and stockings with seams. Ladies, you know what I'm talking about....the legs that seem to just keep going forever? At the time, I was busy looking in shop windows trying to find a present for my best girlfriend, whom we were going to meet in an hour. I wasn't finding anything I liked, and I was going out of my mind with frustration.

I looked over at him, and he was looking at her. In the middle of the street I unloaded on him. "If you could spend a little less time looking at Miss High Heels," I said angrily, "maybe you could help me find something for Betsy!"

My husband turned and stared at me. "I don't know what you're talking about," he said, with an expletive or two thrown in, obviously stung by my tongue-lashing.

And we just stared at each other. I'm sure some of the other pedestrians were staring at us, too, because we were on the verge of a massive fight in the middle of the street.

Suddenly, in a split-second moment, I had to ask myself: do I trust my husband?

Was he telling the truth or lying to cover up the fact that he really was staring at that girl's high heels and long legs?

This question meant *everything* to me. If I didn't trust him, it meant that we had a real problem. The problem wasn't that he looked at her legs. The problem would have been that he *lied* to me about it when I confronted him.

If I *did* trust him, it meant that I had to accept the implication of his statement--that he in fact was *not* ogling her.

I didn't have a lot of time to think the whole thing through. He was staring at me, shocked at my sudden outburst, waiting for me to say something.

And probably some of those other people walking nearby us were waiting, too!

I made the decision. I trusted my husband. Instead of having to repeat or amplify the accusation I'd made, I did something that probably surprised my husband: I retracted it.

I took responsibility for the situation.

Here's how it played out:

"I'm sorry," I said, in much quieter tones. "I guess I'm upset because I need to find a gift and I'm not having any luck, and I apologize for taking my frustration out on you."

He said, "Yeah, you *are* taking it out on me!"

I responded, "And I know you're going to forgive me, because you know how hard it is for me to switch and take responsibility like this, right?"

My husband's features softened as he said, "Of course." The argument was over before it had begun--because I took responsibility for the situation.

The argument was over before it had begun--because I took responsibility for the situation.

What, in fact, was going on? I was upset because I couldn't find a present. I took that frustration out on the man I loved--I lashed out at him. The situation wasn't, "My husband is looking at other women." The situation really was, "I'm unfairly taking my frustration out on my husband."

Once we define a situation accurately, we are able to take responsibility for our role in that situation. And that's when great communication happens.

Incidentally, within five minutes of our almost-altercation, we found the perfect gift for my friend--and we went on to have a wonderful day. All because I stopped in mid-rant, understood what the situation really was all about, and communicated clearly to my husband.

Whenever I tell this story I am always asked, "What if he really *was* ogling that girl?" My answer is this: if he *was* looking at her legs, he has good taste. Just as if we were in a museum with fabulous paintings, I don't expect my husband to look away from beauty. I only request that he do so without others noticing, so that I won't feel embarrassed. I'm actually glad that my husband likes women!

When you're making somebody wrong, that person's *not* going to be on your team. Start taking responsibility to remove the make-wrongs from the way you communicate with others. This takes practice...but I'm sure you'll enjoy working with this new skill, especially when you see the wonderful results you'll create in your life!

By the way, if you don't like the way your partner makes toast, *make it yourself,* instead of making him wrong. In addition, never start a sentence with an accusatory "You always" or "You never" because that *forces* the other person onto the defensive.

It's always a gift to your partner, or whomever you're with, to take responsibility for a situation. In our society today, there's such a lack of people taking responsibility...but somebody has to model it. Why not us? My clients' relationships improve dramatically whenever they remember the magic words: as soon as you own it, you can fix it.

....

As soon as you own it, you can fix it.

....

Let's now turn to the **second problem in communication, the inability to actively listen.** Active listening means two things. First, you get out of your brain and world. Second, you go wholeheartedly to the other person's world, leaving all your judgments and feelings out. Normally, when we listen, we listen from our own perspective. We may *pretend* we're listening, but we're really listening to our own mind as it judges the other person. We feel we know about everything the other person is saying. We're so wise and intelligent about other people that we know what they're going to say halfway through their sentence! And that's why we never even bother *listening* to the second half of most people's sentences--why should we? We're already the world's leading expert on the way they should lead their lives! What could they possibly tell us about themselves that we don't already know?

Obviously this kind of listening, which is all too common, doesn't lend itself to excellent communicating. When we start judging, we're no longer listening. We're simply in our own world. If you can suspend all your judgments while you're listening, communication is exciting and enlivening—because you're open. You can take in what the other person is trying to tell you. Judgment, on the other hand, comes in and shuts you down. We need to abandon the know-it-all approach and listen from the perspective of the speaker. We need to start off by knowing *absolutely nothing* about what they're going to say. When we do this, it's ecstasy! Try it and you'll see!

We need to start off by knowing *absolutely nothing* about what they're going to say. When we do this, it's ecstasy!

When you're working to listen actively, try to avoid judging anything about the person to whom you're listening. This includes their appearance, the way they speak, their attitude, their mannerisms, and everything else. Consciously decide to see and hear them not as a body with a soul, but as a soul with a body. Try not to focus on their hair, their jewelry, or their nose ring. Don't let your ideas or thoughts get in the way. Work to remove the need to insert your own opinion. The rewards of active listening are so powerful that I know you will be extremely happy to practice these skills. You have to make a conscious effort to do active listening, though! You have to call it forth. The more you make yourself practice active listening, the easier it will get. The experience of active listening is usually joyful, elevating, and fun for both the speaker and the listener.

The most common setting for active listening comes when we fall in love. When people are newly in love, they tell you they can finish their partner's sentences, and they can feel exactly how their partner feels. Unfortunately, this doesn't last very long. Why? Because when we first meet someone and are truly interested in what they have to say and who they are, we listen without an agenda, without adding judgment, and we listen from *their* world. This is one of the reasons why we feel such a "high" from those conversations...why time seems transcendent. The hours feel like minutes. We can get a true experience of love for the other person because the other person is actively listening to us and we feel at one with that person. The speaker feels loved and valued by the listener. There are moments with my husband where I am intensely listening to him, and I can actually see him lighten up and have an experience of love for me as a result of my listening. And the same is true the other way around.

The solution to the problem of inactive, or passive, listening is what I like to call "resolution-oriented communication." This is the opposite of seeking to make the other person wrong. Being right and making others wrong alienates people. By the way, letting someone else be right doesn't mean you have to be wrong. It's like the old adage, "There are three sides to every story: yours, mine, and the truth." Let me give you an example of "resolution-oriented communication" in which my client didn't have to make the other person wrong...but she didn't have to be wrong, either. Besides, remember, in most cases, there *is* no right or wrong, but rather, differing perceptions.

Emily is a set decorator whose sister Sandy lives in the same apartment building. Emily described Sandy to me as a thief and a pathological liar. Whenever Emily visited Sandy's apartment, she would find things that belonged to her--jewelry, books, articles of clothing. Emily didn't want to break off the relationship with Sandy, whom she loved despite these negative traits. But Emily was on the verge of despair--and was also on the verge of moving out of her apartment, which she loved, simply to get away from her sister.

I asked Emily to describe the last conversation she'd had with Sandy about Sandy's stealing. Emily told me that last Sunday morning, she'd stopped by Sandy's apartment. There, on Sandy's bed, was a white sweatshirt of Emily's that Emily had been missing for weeks. When Emily asked what her sweatshirt was doing on Sandy's bed, Sandy replied, "I don't know what you're talking about! I didn't take it!"

Emily was going out of her mind over her sister's behavior. I first asked Emily if she wanted to continue to have a relationship with Sandy. She said yes. I then told Emily that we would have to find a way to communicate her feelings to Sandy...*without making Sandy wrong.*

This shocked Emily, because in Emily's mind, Sandy *was* wrong! (It will always feel this way.) Sandy was wrong for stealing, and wrong for lying and claiming that she hadn't taken the sweatshirt. After all, the evidence was in plain sight--the sweatshirt was sitting on Sandy's bed.

This is what I told Emily to say to Sandy: "I really want to have a relationship with you. But what's in the way is our belief system about what's mine and what's yours. I don't want to have to move out of the building. Can you help me with this?"

This kind of conversation-opener moves us toward solution. Instead of making the other person wrong (calling her a liar and a thief), we redefine the situation. The situation is no longer whether Sandy is a liar and a thief. The situation is now result-oriented, in that *Emily* wants Sandy's help in gaining clarity about what belongs to Emily and what belongs to Sandy. Instead of accusing Sandy, Emily is now asking for Sandy's help.

Keep in mind that this approach doesn't always get you the results you want. The other person may not *want* a healthy, honest relationship with you! They may just want to steal your stuff! But at least this way, everybody has to put their cards on the table. Nothing important is left uncommunicated. If there's going to be a relationship of any kind, it can happen when we say, "I'm uncomfortable when my stuff appears in your room," not, "You've been stealing from me for twenty-five years. What on earth is wrong with you?" Remember to ask yourself whether you *really* want a good relationship or whether you just want to make someone else wrong.

....

Remember to ask yourself whether you *really* want a good relationship or whether you just want to make someone else wrong.

....

The situation between Emily and Sandy took a most surprising turn. Sandy actually agreed to come in with her sister for a joint session with me. At the session, Sandy, not surprisingly, took Emily's initial statement as criticism. Why shouldn't Sandy do that? She'd been criticized by everyone she'd ever known for stealing their stuff. So Sandy started off on the defensive.

"I didn't take your stuff," Sandy said.

"How can you say that?" Emily responded calmly. "My sweatshirt was on your bed, and I didn't give it to you. I would have, if you'd asked, but that's not what happened."

146

"I didn't take it," Sandy insisted, but not as defensively now. "I was going to put it back."

This was an "aha" moment for all of us. We had quickly come to the root of the problem. Emily and Sandy defined the word "take" very differently. Emily defined "take" as "remove without permission." Sandy defined "take" as "removing something *without an intention to return it."*

In Sandy's mind, she'd never stolen anything...because anything she "took" she always meant to return. Sandy later admitted that she didn't always get around to returning stuff, and Emily admitted that frequently the stuff Sandy "borrowed without permission" turned up back in her apartment a few days or weeks later. So Sandy and Emily reached a new agreement: that in the future, Sandy would ask permission before she removed anything from Emily's apartment, *regardless of how long Sandy intended to keep it.* We usually fight about things where we don't have an agreement in place. By making an agreement, Sandy and Emily had a way to avoid future arguments over the same thing.

The sisters went away happy. The problem was solved when Emily no longer had a need to make Sandy wrong. If you take a few moments and ask yourself who in your life you've been making wrong, you might be able to fix some long-standing and seemingly unsolvable problems!

....

If you take a few moments and ask yourself who in your life you've been making wrong, you might be able to fix some long-standing and seemingly unsolvable problems!

....

The third problem with communication is that people are unwilling to take responsibility for their lives and everything in their lives, including the results. Nothing can be fixed until we take responsibility. We're powerless if we're blaming others. How do we find the areas where we aren't taking responsibility? We look at our lives. If we find an area where something isn't working the way we want it to work, that's where we probably need to take responsibility.

147

Most communication is not resolution or solution-oriented. As a result, instead of leaving interactions whole and complete, we leave them feeling incomplete and get to hold on to our anger and our "rightness." In order to have communication that works, we have to change the way we *approach* the interaction. Most people go into an interaction with an idea in their heads of how it's going to turn out. They don't realize that they'll *make* that interaction turn out *exactly* the way they envisioned it! Most of this is born from fear. If a young man asks a girl for a date in a very fearful manner, believing she'll say no, do you think there's much chance for his success? Of course not. If we envision the worst, we generally get the worst, again, because we have *rehearsed* it in our head.

Taking responsibility means it's never about blame. My client, James, an attorney, was able to dazzle juries and win cases for his clients...but he couldn't get a word in edgewise with his mother. According to James, every word that came out of his mother's mouth was negative and critical. James's mother declared that James's wife was too skinny, his secretary was rude, his children were borderline hyperactive, and on and on and on. James came to me because he wanted to know how he could help his mother to be less negative.

I explained to him what you and I have just discussed: that rather than distributing blame, the question becomes how do we fix what's wrong. (This was a new one for him, since his whole livelihood *depends* on making other people wrong!) I also explained to him that as long as he's still trying to fix his mother, he's missing the big picture. The big picture is that we can't change other people. We only have real power over our own attitudes, and reactions. The situation couldn't be about his mother's negativity, as James originally thought. Instead, it was important to redefine the situation as *James's discomfort* with his mother's negativity. By taking responsibility and calling it *his* discomfort, now James had a chance to fix it.

There were several possibilities, some of which were: (1) James could set boundaries and limits with his mother. (2) He could spend less time with her if she refused to respect his boundaries. (3) He could schedule some goal-oriented family therapy with his mother. I suggested that he use the following words to make a request of his mother: "Mom, I'm really working on my negativity, and in doing that, I'm not allowing myself to be around negativity. Could you please keep things on a positive note when we're talking?"

This way, James was able to make the whole thing *his* issue rather than hers. His mother was so surprised by his request that she agreed. Six months have passed since James and I first spoke about this, and his mother speaks positively, at least in James's presence, most of the time. She respected his idea after a while, and now actually *catches herself* when she starts criticizing.

Remember, when you make a request, you must always be willing to hear "no." Not everyone who traffics in negativity, gossip, and complaining is going to be ready to give it up. The same is true for anyone you approach about anything--they may just not want to do it your way, and you have to be okay with that when you go into the situation.

The thing I don't understand, incidentally, is why people feel so negative in today's strong economy. What would it take for people to be positive? Most think it's money, but it's not. The thing that would make people feel more positive is *better relationships*, which they can achieve through...you guessed it, better communication skills.

There are a lot of negative people in the world. Old, young, rich, poor--the disease of negativity strikes so many people. It's hard to stay positive in the face of a relentless onslaught of negativity. Take my client Amy, a city planner. Amy had a co-worker who simply wouldn't talk to her. Something Amy had done or said--Amy had no clue what it might have been--didn't sit well with that co-worker, who gave Amy the cold shoulder for more than a year.

Amy came to me quite upset about this, as you can imagine. This co-worker happened to work in the next cubicle from Amy's. The fact that the co-worker wouldn't talk to Amy changed every single working day of Amy's life. As a result of that co-worker's unwillingness to get complete or tell the truth, Amy carried it with her until she hated her job, hated everybody there, and was on the verge of leaving the job. It was even starting to affect other friendships of Amy's. The solution I offered Amy took advantage of the surprising fact that when *we* practice communication skills, we don't always need to hear communication coming back to us from the other person!

When *we* practice communication skills, we don't always need to hear communication coming back to us from the other person!

I told Amy to write a letter to her co-worker explaining exactly how she felt about the situation. I told Amy not to expect any response. By the way, I didn't think it was necessary, under these circumstances, that Amy remove the make-wrong! The point was not to re-enter into a relationship with the co-worker. Amy didn't want that. Amy just wanted to get some completion and some peace of mind. I suggested that Amy include in the letter the phrase, "I refuse to let you take any more of my energy."

The good news is that Amy's co-worker grudgingly admitted that she'd been wrong and now even speaks to Amy once in a while. The better news is that the situation is no longer an energy drain in Amy's life. Thanks to her use of these communication skills, Amy is no longer bothered by whatever her co-worker chooses to do or not do. When we communicate what we truly feel, we are empowered--regardless of what the other person says or does in response.

When we communicate what we feel, we are truly empowered--regardless of what the other person says or does in response.

So there you have it--a new toolbox filled with communication skills ready for your inspection and use. You might ask what a book on eating has to do with communication skills. The answer, of course, is *everything!* Nothing is more depressing than a downward-spiraling relationship. Nothing drives people to the ice cream aisle faster than an inability to express feelings to other people. Communicating helps us get things off our chest instead of getting things into our bellies. In fact, you could sum up this whole chapter in this way:

Open your mouth and speak...so you don't have to open your mouth and eat!

Chapter Eleven -- Anger is Fattening!

The strongest emotion we can experience is anger. Anger helps to keep weight on people. Most people have never learned how to productively discharge their anger, so they keep it inside. And it accumulates. People who one day take out a gun and kill sixteen people in an office building are generally not doing so because one person made them angry one time. They have had a build-up of anger, together with an inability to discharge that anger. They knew no other way of letting go of the anger except by acting out in such a dreadful way.

Continuously holding anger is analogous to taking in air without being allowed to let any air out. Eventually we will explode! And that's how it is with anger. Most of us keep eating our anger because we don't have training on how to let it out properly, and eventually we explode.

....

Most of us keep eating our anger because we don't have training on how to let it out properly, and eventually we explode.

....

When we hold our anger in, we hold onto lots of other things as well, including weight. In this chapter, we are going to focus on how to let go of the anger that traps us in lives that we do not thoroughly enjoy living, and that keeps excess weight locked in our bodies.

First we have to understand that anger is really a cover-up for other things. Often, we become angry because we are actually *fearful* about a situation that has happened. We are fearful because we don't know exactly how we should feel about that situation or what we should do. The biggest reason for this ambiguity is because we are unaware of, or out of sync with, our value system. For this reason, whenever I am working with a client who wants to reduce his or her level of anger, I always ask that client to draw a personal Mission Statement. Businesses use Mission Statements in order to define themselves and to guide their employees. I find that having a personal Mission Statement helps an individual to know exactly how to react to virtually any situation that can come down the pike. When we know what our values are, we won't be shaken or made as fearful by a new situation or a new twist on an old situation. Instead, we can feel more centered about making all of our decisions, since they spring from our underlying values.

....

When we know what our values are, we won't be shaken or made as fearful by a new situation or a new twist on an old situation.

....

I'd like to suggest that you now write your own personal Mission Statement. A few suggestions--the shorter and more concise it is, the better. Also, your personal Mission Statement should be written in the present tense--that is, use powerful statements like "I am," "I do," and "I can." It's best to avoid statements that begin with weaker points of view such as "I wish," "I want," or "I will be." A personal Mission Statement is about who you are right now--or who you want to be right now. If you express it in positive, active terms, you are more likely to find yourself agreeing with and living by that personal Mission Statement.

Here's my own personal Mission Statement: "I am a person who creates joy in other people's lives by being a conduit for transformation."

When situations arise in my life, I test them against this personal Mission Statement. I very rarely find myself in a position where I do not know what to do or how to feel about something that's going on, even if I've never confronted that thing before. That's because my personal Mission Statement grounds me and helps me know who I am in relation to whatever is going on in the world around me.

We've all been asked many times to do things that we don't believe in. Sometimes these things are conspicuously wrong. Other times, these things are neither illegal nor immoral, but just don't feel right. When your value system is firmly in place, you can sense your own answers, sometimes just from the discomfort you feel in making a decision. When you finally do come to a decision based on your values, you usually know it's right, because it feels right. It feels complete. It *feels* like the right thing to do, even though it may not necessarily *look* like it. It is vital for us to know our own values and to live by them. It is also extremely freeing. If you have never written down or even looked at your own value system or Mission Statement, doing this exercise should immediately make you feel better, more at ease, more centered. This is Step One in draining anger from our lives.

Exercise

This is my personal Mission Statement:

_____

_____

_____

_____

_____

Congratulations! You're on your way to having your life make more sense to you, and be much more enjoyable. You might want to transfer this Mission Statement to a spot on your wall for a while, somewhere where you will see it every day, until you feel it's a part of you...a part of your life.

Once we've written our personal Mission Statement, we will have begun to reduce the amount of anger in our lives. Anger is often a product of confusion, fear, and frustration. By knowing who we are and what we want, we can alleviate many of those painful emotions. Let's now turn to the question of what anger is really all about. In order to begin this inquiry, let me ask you a question: have you ever awakened and found yourself trying to remember if you're angry?

Have you ever awakened and found yourself trying to remember if you're angry?

Think back to a time when you had a disagreement with someone close to you, most likely someone in your family. You went to sleep that night angry, you probably didn't have the sweetest of dreams, and then when you awakened the next morning, you actually had to concentrate to remember if the anger you felt was a dream or if you were really angry. Sometimes when we awaken, we don't remember the anger. We get up, we brush our teeth, and suddenly we remember: "Oh, yeah, I'm mad at so and so." In other words, we had to first make a determination that we were angry, and then we had to decide to hold onto it. Can you see how much energy that takes?

Why do we do this? Why do we get angry, and why do we sometimes seek to rouse ourselves into a state of anger that we had pretty much forgotten about? The surprising answer is that anger has payoffs. One of the primary perks, or benefits, of feeling anger, is that we think that having our anger punishes someone! We get to say, at least inside our head, "I'm really mad that you did this to me, and I'm gonna stay mad at you for a long, long time!" We eventually realize that we don't punish the other person with this behavior--we punish ourselves. We punish ourselves because anger takes energy. When we expend energy on anger, we lose out on what's happening in the present.

Much of our self-expression, much of our joy, comes from being present in the moment, alive right now. Anger doesn't allow you to experience the present, because all of our energy gets directed to the anger, which is usually about something that happened in the past. Anger is the Pac Man of emotions because it's bigger, powerful, and more destructive than any other emotion we can feel. It eats up all our good feelings and happy emotions, simply because it's bigger and stronger than anything else in our mind.

Anger can also be an excuse to not try something in life. If we stay frozen in anger at a previous partner or spouse, we can

156

justify to ourselves not trying to meet someone new. So two of the main benefits of anger, if we can really call them "benefits," is that we get to punish, although we only end up punishing ourselves, and that we get to stay frozen in the past, even though this destroys any chance of a happier present or future.

Anger is also strongly related to the need or compulsion to be right. Generally the more insecure we are, the stronger our need to be right. Needing to be right goes hand in hand with needing to feel in control. People who don't feel valued, noticed, or taken seriously become extremely resentful of everyone around them, because they feel that their perceptions and world view are ignored. This is an extremely painful state, and it triggers a lot of anger.

Other people have perceptions and world views of their own, and those people were not put on earth to meet our needs. Since that's the case, we can draw a straight line from low self-esteem, lack of a sense of control, and a need to be right, directly to the development of anger. This sequence can be set in motion by dominating, righteous parents or siblings, an overall feeling of insecurity about one's own intelligence, experience, or worthiness, or many other reasons. The chapter on how to break the addiction to being right will help you understand how to reduce the level of anger you experience in your life. In short, anger is about giving too much weight to our own opinions!

Another very important aspect of anger is the link between anger and the failure to take responsibility for one's actions. When we take responsibility for our actions and the consequences of those actions, then we can discover where and how we are making mistakes. We can learn lessons, and we can fine tune our life. Those who simply live their lives trying to cover up mistakes and present an image of a person who is always right, never get to learn from their experiences. What happens when we lie in order to cover up mistakes we make, instead of taking responsibility for them and letting the chips fall where they may? Once we tell a lie, we have to constantly look over our shoulder and remember what we have said. We may have to tell larger and larger lies in order to protect ourselves. The more we lie, the more we are unable to express ourselves in any meaningful way. When self-expression is gone, what remains is a shell of a person, a mask that the person must wear at all times.

....

When self-expression is gone, what remains is a shell of a person, a mask that the person must wear at all times.

....

The more time passes, and the more lies that are not retracted or handled, the more masks one must wear until who we truly are literally becomes buried under the weight of all those lies. We may not even remember who we were, because the more masks we wear, the more inconsistent we are with our own reality. Life is no longer a real experience, but one with a facade that must be maintained.

The opposite of this downward spiral is a life where we take responsibility for our actions and tell the truth. The more consistently we are our true selves with all the people in our lives, the higher the degree of mental health, comfort, self-esteem, self-assurance, and the more happiness and internal success we are able to enjoy.

People who tell the truth and accept responsibility for their actions can truly be themselves with the important people in their lives. They love being with those people. They know they can confide in loved ones, tell them about their darkest sides, without worrying about feeling judged, criticized, embarrassed, or unworthy. Those who tell the truth and accept responsibility for their actions don't need masks. It follows, then, that the goal is to decrease the number of masks we wear and increase the number of people with whom we can truly be ourselves!

When we do not tell the truth, when we do not take responsibility for our lives, the sad result is more and more anger. We know that we are saying and doing the wrong thing, and our intrinsic sense of right and wrong reminds us that we are not living up to our own expectations. We get angry as a result-- sometimes at ourselves, but usually at everyone else around us.

The word responsibility, on the other hand, can be looked at this way: *response-ability*, or the ability to respond, the ability to choose an appropriate response to any situation. Our ability to choose a response is based on our value system and where we put our energy. If our energy is constantly expended on hiding from ourselves and others, on defending ourselves, on justifying our actions, or on making excuses, then our ability to respond in an honest fashion will be diminished. Instead of responding we will react, and reaction is not communication. In fact, reaction is the biggest obstacle *to* communication. There is no communication at all when one is simply reacting. So how do we get out of reaction and move into communication? The answer is to focus our attention and energy on taking responsibility.

....

How do we get out of reaction and move into communication? The answer is to focus our attention and energy on taking responsibility.

....

People who take responsibility for their lives don't deny that they might have had a problem childhood. They don't deny their genetics, environment, upbringing, or influences. They just use their free will to change those things that they don't like, rather than blame those things for the way their lives are. When we recognize that we have free will, that we are not prisoners of our own prior experience, we can choose the best response, rather than reacting on an instinctual level. The more we practice these skills, the better we get at using them. Although we may experience grief, sorrow, annoyance, or other negative emotions, those emotions will last for only a short time.

If we do not learn to take responsibility, we will stay stuck in our anger and other negative emotions. We will suffer more grief, feel more pain, and spend more time upset. People who are stuck in blame and anger cannot move forward, grow, or change. By taking responsibility for our actions, and by committing to tell the truth, to the best of our ability, we reduce the amount of anger in our lives, and thus we become mentally and physically healthier.

There's also a surprising relationship between living with anger and living *without* integrity. Let me tell you a story from my own life. My husband and I belonged to a gym many years ago that announced that it would be soon closing for good. The gym provided its members small terry cloth towels that we thought were absolutely perfect for workouts. Since the gym was closing anyway, we decided to stuff two of those towels in our gear bags on the last day. Not exactly the act of a person living with integrity!

We used those stolen towels all the time when we were working out or hiking. Four years later, on a hike in the beautiful Sierra Mountains, we were discussing how upset we felt that our housekeeper had somehow managed to misplace those two workout towels. We searched everywhere in our home, but we couldn't find them. At the top of the mountain we were hiking one day, I had an epiphany--we stole those towels, and now someone had taken them from us! This was a very small, low-cost lesson of "what goes around comes around." It was one of those rare, enlightening moments in life. I said to myself, "If you want to know why you're getting what you're getting, look at what you're doing."

From that moment to this, my husband and I have not stolen anything, big or small. We don't want the bad karma that comes from stealing. I'm embarrassed as I tell this story, but I feel it's important to see that we all find ways to justify dishonest behavior. We were living without integrity. The way we live in the small things dictates the way we live in the large things. If the universe cannot trust us with some small terry cloth towels, why should it trust us with anything bigger or more wonderful?

....

If the universe cannot trust us with some small terry cloth towels, why should it trust us with anything bigger or more wonderful?

....

Okay, I've come clean. Now it's your turn. Are you living with complete integrity? Are there areas of your life in which you are not living up to your own expectations about yourself?

The distance--sometimes it's immense--between our expectations of our own behavior and our actual behavior triggers an enormous amount of anger directed at ourselves. If you don't like the level of anger in your life, take a look at your behavior. If it does not measure up to your true expectations of the way people should be in the world (your value system), you may want to change that behavior. Justifying it by saying that it doesn't matter, that everybody does it, or that in the scheme of things it's not that important, doesn't help. We actually have to live with integrity in every aspect of our lives if we want to keep anger from corroding the foundations of our character.

There's a wonderful expression: "A thief lives in fear of being stolen from." If we are willing to sacrifice the feeling of glee that sometimes comes from getting away with something, we can live our lives in a more honest fashion. Thus we will be able to experience true self-expression. The more clean we get with ourselves, the more trust we will be able to put in other people. The more things we do that make us feel good about ourselves, the more comfortable we will feel in the presence of others.

Sometimes when we think about anger, we are actually thinking about our "dark side." The dark side is the part of us that does not measure up to our own expectations. The fact is that all of us have a dark side. We have all sinned. We have all had very bad thoughts. We have all wished terrible things upon other people, even people we love. Yet there is a huge distinction between thinking evil thoughts and taking evil actions. We need to accept the fact that all of us have evil thoughts--it's just simply human nature. We do have the choice not to act on those evil thoughts. The problem begins when we refuse to see or admit the existence of our dark side--when we do evil or sinful things and refuse to recognize them as wrong. It's only when we are able to examine our behavior and recognize when we have acted in a manner that does not match our values that we are able to grow emotionally and spiritually.

I'd like to tell a little story about myself right now. I used to belong to a networking group where several times a month I would meet with other businesswomen. We would discuss the various services we provided, and frequently we would hire each other. On one occasion I met a makeup artist named Sue at one of these meetings. I asked her what she would charge me for a makeup application lesson. She replied, simply and without any qualification, "One hundred fifty dollars." I was truly shocked at her fee and I didn't try to hide my shock. "Wow," I said, and I frankly got away from her as fast as I could.

About a week later, a friend of mine told me that she had met Sue for coffee, and she wanted to know whether I was open to hearing some feedback on how Sue had perceived me. I told her I was open, but somehow I already knew what she was going to say. My friend told me that Sue felt that I didn't value her work, and that she felt insulted by my reaction to her fee. I understood why she felt that way. I knew I had to call Sue and apologize for the brusque way I had treated her.

I wasn't ready to call her yet, because I was still in shock about how much money she charged. I needed a full day before I was ready to take responsibility to see what was really going on. What happened was this: I discovered I was actually jealous of the fact that Sue could quote her fee so clearly and so free of self-doubt. The way she said "one hundred fifty dollars" conveyed the impression that she truly believed she was worth every penny of it. I came to realize that I was jealous because I was never able to just state my fee. I always would follow it up with, "but if you can't afford it, I can lower it!" I never realized that on some level, I did not believe I was worth as much as I was charging. Sue's confidence made me aware of my own lack of confidence.

After this discovery, I called her to apologize for the brusque way I had spoken to her. She was very grateful for the call, and I was very grateful for the lesson I had learned.

Sometimes our dark side can be triggered by emotions like jealousy, envy, or self doubt. Emotions like that have the possibility to destroy relationships with other people, sometimes even before those relationships have a chance to begin, as was the case with Sue and me. It's my job--it's the job of each of us-- to recognize when a "dark side" emotion triggers anger, which can interfere with our ability to live our lives to the fullest.

Coincidentally, a new client called me the very next day and asked me my fee. For the first time ever since I had opened the doors to my office, I was able to state my fee without adding anything self-defeating afterwards! And as soon as I did it, I felt an indescribable sense of bliss, fully recognizing the gift I had received from this experience.

If I had not called Sue and taken responsibility, I would have remained stuck in something like "Well, she has her nerve charging that much money!" And I would have found it difficult to be around her.

Another little *perk* of my taking responsibility was that Sue called me shortly thereafter because she wanted to give me a free make-up session as a result of how touched she was by my phone call.

Whenever we find ourselves repeatedly justifying some action that we took or something that we said, we pay a price in terms of self-expression. Self-expression gets squelched when we are preoccupied on a subconscious level with violations of our own value system. In contrast, when we feel complete with ourselves, or get the gift, we move forward in life, usually with joy.

Along the same lines, it is necessary for us to give up feeling or creating guilt. One reason is that guilt can become a standard way of dealing with shame or perceived wrongdoing in many families. The deeper reason is that sometimes people feel that as long as they feel guilty for doing something, they are exonerated for what they did. They are absolved from needing to take responsibility for their action, or apologizing for it, or even for changing. As long as people feel guilty, they can tell themselves they've already paid the price, and they can get away with it. Trying to *place* guilt on others is also very destructive. When we cause people to feel guilty about their actions, we are actually helping them down a road toward failing to take responsibility for what they do. They will be immersing themselves in guilt, rather than constructive action. Guilt is really believing that you are not living up to someone else's expectations of you. Well, sometime in your life, you are going to have to accept that you *can't* live up to others' expectations of you. You can only meet your own expectations.

....

Guilt is really believing that you are not living up to someone else's expectations of you.

....

Sometimes anger, whether directed at ourselves or at other people, is a function of having faulty perceptions. Consider the newborn child, who has no perceptions. As infants progress through their first year, they experience successes and failures at expressing themselves and trying to get their needs met. Soon they will try to walk. They may stumble at first, fall, or land on different parts of their bodies. Infants at that point don't think, "Gee, I failed...I'll never try that again!"

No. The child gets up and keeps trying, most times with laughter. A child that young hasn't been taught how to feel inadequate or guilty about efforts and errors. Sometimes, however, adults give negative reactions, both verbally and non-verbally, to children. Thus they *learn* to feel inadequate, wrong, bad, stupid, and afraid. The more traumatic the experience--the stronger the negative reaction from others, the more indelible the perception. Infants subjected to this negativity will begin to form negative beliefs and thoughts about themselves and others. Amazingly, those negative perceptions formed in infancy can last a lifetime. A cycle is set in place that causes the individual to look at the negative side of life. In other words, images and thoughts create feelings, and those feelings create behavior. If the images and thoughts with which we are presented are negative, we will have negative feelings about ourselves, and we will act negatively. And not surprisingly, we will be angry at the results. That's why it's important to examine the perceptions we hold about ourselves and our lives, so that we no longer find ourselves limited by negative thought patterns we developed at earlier points along the way.

Anger, worry, and fear are inextricably intertwined. I have heard worry and fear described as "tragic misuses of the imagination." I love that description, because I think it is perfect. Worry and fear are invented--they are made up! We literally create worry and fear out of nothing. Why do we do it?

There are several reasons. First, many people are taught to fear. Was your mother a worrier? Did most of her sentences begin with "What if...?" Was your father, your grandmother, or a sibling a worrier? Many of us are simply taught how to worry growing up at home. Second, have you, for any number of reasons, always tried to be perfect? It's easy to see how this could create lots of worry and fear for a person, because there is no such thing as perfect! Are you always trying to keep from making a mistake? This, too, causes much worry, since mistakes in life are inevitable, and are actually great learning experiences. John Wooden, the great basketball coach at UCLA, used to tell his players that "whichever team makes the most mistakes wins." It's also said that "a life spent making mistakes is far more honorable than a life doing nothing."

....

John Wooden, the great basketball coach at UCLA, used to tell his players that "whichever team makes the most mistakes wins." It's also said that a life spent making mistakes is far more honorable than a life doing nothing."

....

Sometimes we create worry and fear because of traumas we've experienced, especially early in life. For example, the death of a parent, close friend, or relative, can scare us so much that we constantly fear other losses. There are many more reasons why you might become a worrier. Whatever the reason, understand that this too falls under the category of being a conversation with yourself that you need to change. Worry and fear are simply conversations that we make up in our heads-- inaccurate perceptions--and this is where we again need to implement the concept of changing our thoughts.

Think about all the things you worry about and fear...how many of them have actually happened? Generally, people respond to me by saying "none" or "very, very few." In fact, the acronym for fear is "False Evidence Appearing Real." So here's what you need to realize about worry and fear. If something does happen and 99% of fears *don't* actually happen, you will have to deal with it then. You don't have to create it now. In fact, don't create it at all. Any time you spend worrying today about something that never is going to happen is time and energy that you will never be able to retrieve. Next, if you're going to change any of your conversations, make one of your new ones, "whatever happens to me, I know I will get through it...successfully." This is what I suggest you do with worry and fear. Turn your fear statements around. It is truly possible to live your life without worry and fear! Remember, it is all made up! It's not real!

To sum up, there are so many ramifications of anger. When we feel angry at ourselves and the world, we don't set goals. We can't tolerate mistakes--our own or those of others. We don't listen to our body. We don't face our addictions. We don't exercise. We don't understand stress and where it comes from. We don't fight fair with the people we love, or try to love. In short, anger is fattening! We hold onto all the things in our life that make us unhappy...and we spend our time suppressing all that anger with constant trips to the refrigerator or the dessert table.

As this chapter has indicated, that's no way to live. I hope that you will consider this chapter an invitation to release the anger that may have dominated your life, or large parts of your life, up until now, so that you can be finally free to enjoy all the beauty and pleasure that life offers. And you'll be able to enjoy life in that brand-new body of yours, the one that automatically seeks and finds its natural weight, without great effort on your part. Release from anger, and then watch the excess pounds melt away, as you start to feel joy again.

Exercise

Take some time now and make the following lists. Please use extra sheets of paper, because this is just a model for how to get started.

With Whom Am I Angry?	What Action Can I Take To Resolve my Anger Or The Dispute?
_____	_____
_____	_____
_____	_____
_____	_____
_____	_____
_____	_____
_____	_____
_____	_____
_____	_____
_____	_____
_____	_____

Tools For Reducing Anger

Here are some very effective tools for reducing the level of anger in your life. When you find yourself getting angry...

1. Cool off from your anger. Give yourself time to think before reacting.

2. Ask yourself, "What's the REAL upset?" It's never really anger. Here's a list of possibilities for what you'll find underneath your anger:

Hurt/Sadness

Fear
Frustration
Disappointment (based on expectations)
Indignation in response to a perceived injustice
Feeling out of control...victimized
Faulty belief systems

Remember, it's vital to get to the *real* emotion under the anger, so that you can do something about it.

3. Ask yourself if you are really angry with *yourself*. The answer is usually Yes.

4. Then ask, "How can I take responsibility for the problem and/or for the solution to the problem?" Or, "How can I take control...or complete, or handle, or finish what's going on?"

5. *Understand* and *hear* the other person's perspective. Remember, expression with true understanding allows the upset to start dissipating almost immediately.

6. Always have your voice be lower and calmer than the other person's, unless you are acting to avoid abuse. This keeps moving things back to calmness.

7. Express yourself responsibly. Expression doesn't mean making the other person wrong, or that you "dump" information on the other person.

8. Understand that you do not have to take things personally.

9. Give up expectations. Instead, learn how to make requests and agreements...without anger.

10. Make sure you have support systems in which you can express your dark side safely--to discharge anger appropriately and move forward.

11. Ask yourself, "What ACTION do I need to take...for now and for the future, to avoid future anger about this issue and/or similar problems?"

I know...I'm giving you a lot to think about. But you don't have to change overnight. (No one can.) By applying these ideas to your life, little by little, you'll find that your anger diminishes...and so will your waistline!

Chapter Twelve -- Self-Esteem: The Ultimate Decision

Why is self-esteem so important? Why, of all the creatures on earth, is it that human beings are the only ones concerned with self-esteem? The answer is because human beings possess the quality of being able to reason and reflect, and to make choices based on that reasoning and reflection. And even more important, human beings are forced to take their minds with them wherever they go.

We can hide from others. We have numerous acts that we use on different people. Sometimes the acts become so ingrained that we cease to be aware of anything but our act. We can forget what is real. I have seen this on many occasions where people start lying when they're young and never stop. They soon cease to be in touch with reality, even when they are all alone. This is where self-esteem becomes so important. The person who is hiding from others with his act unfortunately cannot hide from himself. The mind goes with us everywhere, and when a person is alone, that is when he or she is most likely to know that the act is just an act, and their self-esteem will suffer.

Self-esteem is a sense of self-efficacy, a sense of regard for one's self and one's abilities, a sense of knowingness that we are appropriate to the world around us, appropriate to reality and to our own life.

....

Self-esteem is a sense of self-efficacy, a sense of regard for one's self and one's abilities, a sense of knowingness that we are appropriate to the world around us, appropriate to reality and to our own life.

....

We need to know that the choices we make in life are good choices, appropriate choices, competent choices. Since we tend to build on this sense of rightness or self-esteem, we have to develop a foundation somewhere. Most people's sense of self-esteem emanates from their childhood and how their parents did or did not let them know of their "okayness." If we did not receive proper mirroring from our parents, as is the case for so many people, then our sense of self-esteem will have started out in a fragile and tentative manner. Quite often, a child with a shaky start at self-esteem will have a poor foundation on which to build self-esteem later in life. How many school courses, after all, have you seen that really teach self-esteem?

Self-esteem is quite distinct from inflated self-regard or boastfulness, which, in fact, are covers for low self-esteem. High self-esteem does not need to express itself. It is comfortable in its knowingness, as opposed to needing to prove itself. Someone with low self-esteem must constantly prove himself, since he is the one who doesn't believe that he is okay. A person with high self-esteem can handle criticism, can make mistakes, and can see the humor in life. He is able to admit his own humanness and can change, grow, and alter his behavior at any time because he is not threatened by this humanness. Such a person will seek out other people with high self-esteem because he is comfortable with others, not threatened by them. He sees the beauty and magnificence of life, and is generally happy as a result of seeing the joys of living a full life.

Conversely, people with low self-esteem seek out others with like qualities, because the quality of feeling threatened, of having prejudices, and complaining, are all a function of not feeling okay with one's self. When we do not feel okay in our conversations with ourselves (another way of describing low self-esteem), we generally feel that it is others who prevent us from having what we want in life. Low self-esteem is also a sure indicator of someone who is unable to take responsibility for what he or she lacks.

Many people with low self-esteem find solace in groups of people who make others wrong for the state of our world, such as hate groups. In this way, they feel a warped sense of self-esteem in having other people around them who have similar feelings and the same need to blame others. They get their sense of self-worth from their likeness to others. And even if they didn't hate a certain group of people before, they will grow to

172

hate that group, and will swear they always did, because that is how they now justify their new, more powerful self.

I once worked with a seven year old client who told me of sexual abuse she suffered at the hands of her grandfather. Her parents refused to believe her, because no one could believe that such an "honorable" man as the grandfather could do such a thing. It was years before the truth ever came out, and only when the grandfather was dying of cancer and wanted to clear his conscience. Grandfather was able to fool lots of people, including his own family, but he had one thing that he had to take with himself everywhere...his mind. He could deny the truth to everyone but himself. So what do you think happens when you carry something inside yourself this toxic? Remember, it has to go somewhere! Sometimes it manifests itself in disease (note that the word disease actually breaks down as dis-ease, a sense of dis-ease with oneself). When one is that much at dis-ease with one's self, how can that person possibly be happy? The mind won't permit it!

Self-esteem is a direct product of the congruity of one's behavior to one's value system. If there is no value system, then congruity is impossible, and what probably exists is a person who continually questions himself--or is a psychopath. It is congruity with one's value system that allows us to feel secure with ourselves, to have a high sense of self-esteem, to be able to feel and express true joy in life, and thus to be able to give love to others.

The question then becomes how does one develop a high sense of self-esteem? I believe it begins with having a value system firmly in place. That's why the Mission Statement I asked you to draft earlier is so important. If you do have a value system in place, but you are not experiencing joy in life, you might want to assess how complete you are with the things that have happened in your life. This includes the issue of forgiveness and making amends to people where needed. It is never too late to assess what we have done in our lives, to make a list of wrongdoings (twelve step programs refer to this as "inventory"), and then to make restitution for those things. In this way, we can move forward and create for ourselves a high self-regard, based on becoming the person we really want to be, and thus becoming congruent with our value system.

In my own life, having at one time been a drug addict (marijuana, diet pills, and sleeping pills), I had experienced a complete incongruence with my value system. As I made reparation and restitution for so many of the terrible things I did, I remember my best girlfriend asking me, "When are you going to forgive yourself?"

At the time, I thought her question to be absurd. I answered, "I don't know." She then told me it was about time...that I was no longer the same person I was then, and that I deserved to forgive myself. I wish I could say that was it, and I subsequently developed my self-esteem, but truth be known, it took me several more years before I could truly forgive myself. I had more apologizing to do and I needed time to truly believe that I had changed for good. This is what I mean when I say that we take our mind with us everywhere. We can deny things to others, but when we're alone, we're alone with our own mind, and from that we cannot hide.

Some people have learned how to hide from themselves, by lying constantly, because the truth is too intolerable to live with. We call this pathology or disease. Once a person has moved into this stage, he will forever have great difficulty with determining what is real and what is not. I spend no time on this because of a personal disdain for selfish and self-centered people who need to turn life around their way to make it fit for themselves. Pathological individuals are rarely good candidates for therapy.

....

Some people have learned how to hide from themselves, by lying constantly, because the truth is too intolerable to live with. We call this pathology or disease.

....

To the extent that we are inauthentic with ourselves, we have inauthentic relationships. As long as we are putting on an act for others, how can we let them get close? Indeed, the whole purpose of putting on an act is to keep people at a distance, usually because we don't want to risk them knowing too much about us and our foibles. How can we expect that our relationships with others will be meaningful or even real, when we fail to be our real self in that relationship? When we develop a sense of self-esteem, feeling congruent with our value system, we also become authentic in our dealings with others. This authenticity allows us to experience life with enthusiasm and joy, since there is nothing for us to do...all we have to do is *be*. Those joys feed on themselves and proliferate. It's almost as if life starts to say to us, "Yes, you're now really okay, and now you get to enjoy and partake in life's pleasures."

I think that the most important decision we will ever make in our lives is the decision of who we are in relationship to the world. The level of self-esteem we feel dictates the way everything in our life will flow. Everybody talks about the importance of self-esteem. Teachers try to give it to their students; bosses, at least in theory, try to give it to their employees; parents want to give it to their children. And yet, we live in a time when so many of us do not look to ourselves in order to determine our intrinsic value. Instead, we look to others. All too often, people truly believe that they are their work, they are their bank account, they are the car they drive, they are their relationship. They never stop to think that outside forces really cannot measure our true worth. Self-esteem means very simply that the self, not outsiders, does the esteeming. Many people (especially women) ask me, "What about being humble? I was taught to be humble." A great answer for this comes from an old saying: "Humble people don't think less of themselves. They just think about themselves less."

In the course of my work, I have discovered twenty keys to self-esteem that make all the difference in my life, and have made measurable, powerful differences in the lives of my clients. I know that when you learn these twenty keys and apply them daily, everything in your life is going to improve. Your relationship with food and your ability to reach and maintain your natural ideal body weight will come effortlessly once these twenty keys are in place in your life. At the same time, it is impossible for us to raise our level of self-esteem without also raising the quality of our personal lives, our love relationships, our family relationships, our success at work, and our financial success. Self-esteem is truly the rising tide that lifts all boats. When we incorporate all of these twenty keys in our lives, we are at peace, and we operate at peak performance as well. It's important to remember that life is also about making mistakes and having setbacks, so applying the twenty keys is truly a lifetime balancing job. Let's take a look at these twenty keys to self-esteem.

Keys to Self-Esteem

1) **Begin by de-emphasizing material possessions.** They don't love you, comfort you, or bring you great joy. They are just things. Try to detach from the "I'll be happy when I have _____" mentality. Here's how you can know for certain that possessions don't really make you happy. Ask yourself how long the thrill lasts when you do acquire something new. A day? An hour? A month? How long before you're on to the next "Now I want to buy a _____"? Corporate America has a multi-billion dollar interest in helping you believe that you're not okay until you own the right cell phone, the right Mercedes, or even the right athletic shoes. As children in this society, we learned early on to keep needing more things to acquire, rather than learning how to be satisfied right now. As a friend of mine says, I used to use people and love things. Now I love people and use things. Things have their place--they're wonderful, but they do not bring happiness.

2) **Stop comparing yourself to others.** Comparing sets you up to feel that you're not enough. If you must compare yourself to others, compare yourself to yourself. Ask yourself whether your life is better today than it was twenty years ago.

Incidentally, when we compare ourselves with others, we always pick people who are doing better than ourselves. It's very rare that someone comes to me as a client and says, "I saw this homeless guy on the street, and boy my life is ten times better than his." We generally look at people who are further up the socio-economic ladder so that we can make ourselves feel bad by comparing our lives to theirs. But the fact remains that we really know nothing about how other people's lives truly are. Let me give you an illustration of this concept.

Not long ago, I was out to dinner and I ran into a client of mine and his wife. This man came to me because of a nine year affair he *thought* he had been conducting behind his wife's back. The affair was destroying his peace of mind, his finances, his business, and his marriage--his wife sensed that another woman was in the picture, although she didn't know the specifics about the affair, and she was contemplating leaving him. I had never met my client's wife prior to this chance encounter in a restaurant. When I saw them together, they looked so happy, well-groomed, well-to-do and together that I had trouble reconciling what I knew about their marriage with the picture they presented. When Shakespeare wrote, "All the world's a stage," he wasn't kidding. So often, the picture that people present of themselves to the outside world is nothing more than theater. And yet we so often accept the picture we see as reality, and then we compare our lives to that false picture, making ourselves feel bad and *less than* others. The simple message is stop comparing yourself to others for two important reasons. First, you have no idea what others' lives are truly like. And second, comparing always sets you up for failure. There is always someone taller, thinner, richer, and more accomplished, *if you're looking for it.*

3) **Resolve to accept yourself unconditionally.** God, or if you are more comfortable, the universe, does not create junk. The way you are is perfect in your Creators' eyes, so why should you have higher standards for yourself than your Creator does? There may be parts of your life that you don't approve of. That's okay. If you have some cleaning up to do or stuff to fix, get to it. As we have seen earlier, unresolved stuff stays with you forever. Then, after an inventory and the appropriate amends or completion work, no matter what you've done in the past, forgive yourself and move on. My clients often come into their initial sessions with a load of guilt appropriate to murderers. Of course they have done nothing anywhere near as terrible as that, and yet

they flagellate themselves as if they had committed the world's most heinous crimes.

Remember that you are the only you in the world. Accept that you are also the best that you can be, and as such, you are a work in progress. Accept your weaknesses as well as your strengths. And if there is still part of you that hates certain things about you, ask yourself if you can love the part of you that hates you.

4) Forgive others for all the things you're still holding onto. Forgiveness does NOT mean that what the other person did was okay, that it was right, that the person shouldn't be punished, that you are condoning their actions, or that you are reconciling the relationship with that person. It simply means that you are choosing to let go of your feelings of resentment and revenge, forever, in favor of moving forward. Punishment may well be appropriate for the behavior of the other person. If we want to be happy, however, we must surrender our badge and gun. We have to leave justice to the professionals. We are not cops. If you happen to be a law enforcement officer, that's great. But try not to take your work home with you! We have to forgive other people not for their sake but for ours.

5) Find your gift or passion and pursue it. Everyone has a gift or gifts. Yours might be for singing, art, candy-making, teaching children, the business world, or something entirely different. Find out what it is that gives you passion, and pursue it. As Oliver Wendell Holmes wrote, "Most people die with their music still in them." Don't let that happen to you. Sometimes people say, "I'd like to go back to school and get that degree, but I'll be thirty eight years old by the time I finish." Well, you'll be thirty eight years old, anyway, right? So why *not* fulfill your dream?

6) Set goals. First get clear on your value system. What matters to you? What kind of person do you want to be? Where do you want to devote your time, effort, and attention? Once you are clear on your value system, your goals will spring forth almost automatically. Goals give us direction, purpose, and reason to celebrate ourselves. They also allow us to have our dreams come true. Give up the failure mentality. Remember that there is no such thing as failure, except in our own minds. "Give me a stock clerk with a goal," J.C. Penney used to say, "and I will give you a man who will make history. Give me a man without a goal, and I will give you a stock clerk." What are you aiming for?

7) **Celebrate your accomplishments, the attainment of your goals, and your successes.** Learning to acknowledge yourself is vital. We have certainly learned how to beat ourselves up! Only acknowledgment actually moves us forward. On a subconscious level, if you do not reward yourself for the wonderful accomplishments and attainments that you are now creating, some part of you will say, "I did all this work--and I got nothing to show for it!" Buy yourself a present, have yourself a trophy or a plaque made up, or find some other meaningful way to acknowledge the successes that you have created. Those tangible signs of success will spur you on to even greater heights.

8) **Reset your goals.** Many people, once they have achieved a goal, sit back and decide to rest, relax, and say, "Okay, I did it." Unfortunately, there is something about human nature that is not content to sit on its laurels. We usually feel hollow if we achieve a goal and then fail to set a new one. We ask ourselves, as did Alfie in the famous song, "Is that all there is?" You want to keep at least one important goal in front of you at all times. In fact, the more goals you have, the better. You might want to only focus on a small number of important goals at one time, though, in order to avoid overwhelm.

9) **Find a way to take responsibility for all your actions and consequences.** Understand that until you accept the idea that you are responsible for the actions you take, you will find yourself constantly feeling victimized, out of control, and overly burdened. A sense of responsibility gives us control over our

lives. We need to understand that we always have choice. You want to give up forever the notion of being a victim of your circumstances, your relationships, your career, or anything else. Replace your sense of victimhood with a sense of being a creator.

....

Replace your sense of victimhood with a sense of being a creator.

....

10) **Work on your communication skills.** The best definition I ever heard of communication is this: looking inside ourselves to see how we feel about something; expressing those feelings to another person; and then being quiet and listening to the other person's response. If we do not learn to communicate, we will simply stuff our emotions, gather up and store anger, and eventually question what is and is not real. Communication skills allow you to turn criticism into requests and to express yourself without alienating others. This must also include setting boundaries. When we set boundaries, we teach people how to treat us!

11) **Tune in to your personal integrity.** Everyone's sense of what is right and wrong is personal, but your body will tell you as well. Start listening to the messages that your body gives you. When you're doing something that you know is wrong, your body will send a strong signal to you. Start tuning those signals in instead of suppressing them or stuffing them with food or other substances or behaviors. Tune in to what is right for you, so that your actions are congruent with who you are, and with your values.

12) **Start investigating and questioning belief systems.** Those who know it all have nothing they can learn. Give up sentences like "I've always been this way," "I can't do that," or "I wish I was someone who..." Self-talk like this simply locks in your belief system. You become what you believe about

yourself. You attract into your life what you believe is possible and you always get what you expect--no more and no less!

13) **Learn to have proper conversations with yourself.** The conversations we conduct with ourselves usually reflect our belief systems. If we focus on being worried, fearing failing, or the what ifs, we are simply beating ourselves down with negativity. Instead, speak positively and visualize positively. As a friend of mine says, instead of focusing on "what if, what if, what if..." focus on "what is, what is, what is." You'll find that your "what is" is pretty darn good, if you will only open your eyes to see just how good your life truly is right now. Create conversations with yourself where you tell yourself things like, "I love to exercise," or "I am adept at everything I do," or "I love to risk." When you have proper conversations with yourself, you will respond in amazing new ways.

Along the same lines, be grateful. End each day by writing down three things for which you're grateful. This is switching yourself from thinking about what you don't have to thinking about what you do have. It's not Pollyanna thinking, but rather directing your mind to a place where good feelings reside. Remember, you're always having a conversation with yourself anyway. Why should it lean toward the negative? Feeling grateful takes practice, especially if you're more inclined to notice what you believe is missing in your life.

14) **Create and nurture love and support systems.** If you don't have solid, loyal friends, it is important to create such friendships. Everyone needs people to talk to and trust in addition to their spouse. As we get older, it seems harder to create friends, but it's not! It just takes effort and trial and error. It is also important to have good advisors in life--therapists, mentors, someone to whom we can turn for advice, since none of us is an expert at everything.

15) **Take care of yourself.** This includes vigilant exercise, proper nutrition, stress education, and yearly physical exams. Make sure your body supports your mind.

16) **Challenge yourself, take risks, grow.** Part of creating self-esteem is feeling adept. When you try something new, challenge yourself to something different or keep going after you miss the mark a few times, you build your self-esteem enormously. Each experience, when you take a risk or try to grow, builds on itself, so that you can call forth this new level of self-esteem to reinforce yourself at any time.

....

Each experience, when you take a risk or try to grow, builds on itself, so that you can call forth this new level of self-esteem to reinforce yourself at any time.

....

17) **Press through fear.** Each time you experience fear and do the fearful thing anyway, you build self-esteem. Fear is simply a signal that you're truly alive. Every time you press through the fear, you've exhibited courage. Courage is a primary building block of self-esteem. A great quote I heard was "Courage is simply fear that has said its prayers."

18) **Handle your incompletions.** It is important to become aware of, and take action on any incompletions outstanding in your life. We've discussed this elsewhere in greater detail, so let's simply recall here that incompletions drain our energy and cause us to repeat unpleasant situations over and over again-- with a concomitant loss of self-esteem with each new repetition of the cycle. Instead of letting those incompletions drain us, we can take action. Action can include education, classes, or what I call growth groups; it can involve either individual or group therapy; or it can involve promises to ourselves, as in, "I'll return to school myself when the kids start high school." The energy we gain from tackling incompletions is so massive that we feel we can do almost anything.

19) **Be willing to give up being right.** Needing to be right is a full-time job and a needless waste of energy. As we have discussed, it is human nature for the mind to want to be right. So be sure to ask yourself exactly what you need to be right about.

Are some of those beliefs about being right holding you back in life? Take another look at the chapter on being right and see what you can let go of and replace with more powerful, positive beliefs.

20) **Laugh at yourself.** Since we have already given up . being right, the next step is to accept ourselves and our humanness. It is utterly silly to take life so seriously when we have such a limited amount of time on earth with which to enjoy ourselves. Laugh as much as possible every day, especially at yourself. The less seriously you take yourself, the less seriously you'll take everyone and everything else. You'll live longer--and you'll live a lot more happily, too.

Chapter Thirteen -- Summing Up

We've come a long way together in a very short time! I'd like to salute you for your courage to read this book all the way through to the end. Have you done all the exercises I offered? I sure hope so! I've spent a lot of time working with clients who struggled with one diet after another until they finally gave Un-Dieting a try. They came to learn that going on a diet is practically the only way to *guarantee* weight gain. They realized that if they approached food differently--the way I've outlined it for you in the first four chapters of the book--they would never need another diet for the rest of their lives.

As we've seen, it's not just what we eat...*it's what's eating us*. Some of the reasons that we hang on to excess fat in our bodies are because of how we're living, how we're treating ourselves and others, how we're communicating, and how we're handling experiences from our past. What we don't complete we must carry with us...in many ways!

I've shared with you techniques for bringing forgiveness into your life, for discharging anger that might otherwise take you back to over-eating, for communicating your wants and needs clearly to your partner, your children, and everyone else in your life. We've discussed the concept of incompletions and we've seen how to resolve, with a minimum of stress or pain, the untreated areas of our lives that still need attention today. We've talked about how there are no forbidden foods, and that you need to weigh and measure neither yourself nor anything you eat. The Food/Fuel Tank gives you a new approach to knowing how much and when to eat. My comments about exercise and about throwing away your bathroom scale are freeing to my clients, and I hope they are freeing to you. We've seen how to escape the high cost of needing to be right. And we've seen the importance of self-esteem, especially as it relates to eating, and the twenty keys to developing self-esteem that we discussed.

By letting go of anger, by making the choice to forgive, by handling your incompletions, by communicating your needs and wants, and by using the new eating concepts we discussed in this book, you will become happier, healthier, and more satisfied with life. You will no longer struggle with weight, and you'll no longer be obsessed with food. You will reach your natural ideal weight without struggle, without diets, without depriving yourself of so-called forbidden foods...and without the need to self-destruct by gaining back all the weight that melted away through Un-Dieting. As you keep talking to yourself in the mirror (this must be a *daily* process), telling yourself how incredibly beautiful you are, inside and out, you will eventually begin to see that you've been depriving yourself of self-inflicted love...something that has actually been available to you all along. Instead, you bought into the *very successful* marketing strategy that has so many Americans feeling like they're not okay unless they look like the images of people on magazine covers.

When you have become free from your obsessions with food, you will experience vastly increased self-esteem, and delight in your vastly improved relationships. I'm convinced that Un-Dieting and all the ideas we've discussed will change your life forever--if you'll let them. I hope that you'll give this a try, and I hope that you'll write or e-mail me (undieting@aol.com) and let me know about the changes in your life. I am excited for you and for all your future success! Best wishes!

About the Author

Jackie Jaye-Brandt is a Corporate Communications Specialist/Organizational Psychotherapist and Lecturer. She holds Bachelor's and Master's Degrees in Psychology and is a licensed Psychotherapist with a private practice in Universal City, California. She is a key speaker for the Motion Picture and Television Fund Wellness Program, lecturing on: *Communications Skills, Stress Management, Self-Esteem, Making Relationships Work, Reducing Anger, Overcoming Fear, Time Management, Finding your Passion,* and *The Power of the Mind.* She has provided training and motivational services to a vast array of companies, including Warner Bros., The Walt Disney Co., Disney Imagineering, Fox Sports, Pritikin, Budget Rent-A-Car, and Harbor-UCLA Medical Center.

Printed in the United States
883900001B